The Mechanics of Independence

PATTERNS OF POLITICAL AND ECONOMIC
TRANSFORMATION IN TRINIDAD AND TOBAGO

The MIT Press
Cambridge, Massachusetts, and London, England

The Mechanics of Independence

PATTERNS OF POLITICAL AND ECONOMIC
TRANSFORMATION IN TRINIDAD AND TOBAGO

A. N. R. Robinson

ISBN 0 262 18044 8 (hardcover)

Library of Congress catalog card number: 77-107995

Dedicated to the young people of the Caribbean
and young people everywhere who struggle for
a more just and humane world.

With the severance of their chief colonial ties in the late 1950s, the territories of the Caribbean became the last major area of the world to reap the political benefits of the upheavals that resulted from World War II. However, after centuries of having their treasures drained by metropolitan overseers, these states have discovered the road of independence to be indeed a rough one. First relegated to roles of watering spots, tax havens, and sources of cheap raw materials, they now find themselves in the uncomfortable position of links—or potential links—in a number of mutually hostile chains of security. The emergence of Fidel Castro in Cuba and Cheddi Jagan in Guyana; military interventions by U.S., Dutch, and British forces; and recent political changes, such as those in Peru and Chile, have all combined to exacerbate already trying conditions. Thus integration of the territories of the area, perhaps the only hope for a visible future, seems nearly as remote now as it did during the heyday of externally imposed isolation.

Still, the future of the area holds as much hope as its recent past held cause for dismay. Each of the various territories has at times shown enough political, economic, and social acumen to convince the interested onlooker that with very small amounts of "no-strings" aid, patience, and understanding, the area could find its way to some kind of effective union.

No nation offers greater insight to both the expectations and the fears for the Caribbean than Trinidad and Tobago. With a genuinely multiracial population and multicontinental cultural traditions and influences, it provides a means of understanding not only the Caribbean but the so-called "third world" in general. And despite the disordered and dangerous conditions of the recent past, the prospects for eventually solving the problems that caused them are not at all gloomy. The people of Trinidad and Tobago, unlike those of many other nations, are fully aware of the courses—and fates—open to them; during my numerous visits to the country I have been particularly struck by the intelligence of the younger generation in assessing the nation's problems.

No one exemplifies this trait better than the author of this book—the Honorable A. N. R. Robinson. We met at Oxford, where we were both ushers in the Oxford Union. For those unfamiliar with this institution, it is a debating society that dates back to Gladstone's days; an usher is a potential debater. But while I proceeded to the task of becoming an intellectual spectator, Ray Robinson was transforming himself into an activist thinker.

Having been almost morbidly concerned with world affairs over the past twenty years, I find it difficult to muster enthusiasm over any work on the subject. This book is an exception. It shows a *way*. It is easy to speculate on possible outcomes to a crisis; it is another thing to delve into the maze of options and emerge with an answer. Robinson has succeeded in transcending the trivial. There are other books, but this is the first that reaches the core of the matter.

This work should prove itself a handbook on both the political and economic aspects of the mechanics of independence. Understanding is firmly rooted in historical perception, and projections are based on an insider's view that only a cabinet minister could obtain; and Ray, aside from having been deputy leader of the country's strongest political party, served as Minister for External Affairs and Minister of Finance and also acted as Attorney General and filled in for the Prime Minister when he was out of the country. It must be realized how difficult it is for one who has held high office to subject himself and his deeds to in-depth evaluation. This book combines the realms of thought, action, and hope.

It is to be hoped that the analysis contained in this work will help allay fears and suspicions and show that there is a way in which rational people rationally solve problems. It is an inside story, one that comes from within, inside the people and from within one man's being. In the final analysis, politics is only as good as the people who make it. Raymond Robinson and his book have something to teach the older countries: that from fledgling republics can arise the intellects and leaders who are both practical and deep enough to solve their problems. All they need is peace.

Robert K. Woetzel
Boston, Massachusetts

In 1953 British troops landed in the British colony of Guiana (which as Guyana became independent in 1966) and overthrew the government of Dr. Cheddi Jagan, a Marxist elected by full adult franchise. The Cuban missile crisis flared in 1962. In the following year U.S. President Lyndon Johnson ordered troops to the Dominican Republic to prevent the return to power of ex-President Juan Bosch. In 1968 British military forces landed on the tiny island of Anguilla to nullify its declaration of separation from the islands of St. Kitts and Nevis. In 1969 Dutch marines moved into the little Dutch colony of Curaçao to "restore order" following labor disturbances with racial undertones. On April 22, 1970, United States warships entered the territorial waters of Trinidad and Tobago amid social and political unrest.

These interventions were, of course, only the more vivid manifestations of the interplay of social, political, and economic forces in the Caribbean. Moreover, events since the Second World War merely telescope the pattern that has prevailed in varying forms since the arrival of Columbus in 1492.

As much as anywhere else in the world, the Caribbean has been an area of international rivalry and social and political conflict. This, however, is only the negative side of the picture. On the positive side, the area, perhaps more than any other in the world, is rich in its experience of social, political, and economic forms, ideas, and institutions.

The calamity is that neither we in the Caribbean nor those outside whose activities impinge on ours have been able so far to make any significant use of this experience. Perhaps the most important reasons for this are the stifling effects of the colonial environment, the tendency of newly independent countries to discount as irrelevant anything associated with the colonial past, and the fact that almost nowhere outside the Caribbean is there a perception of area identity.

The second reason given is the most understandable. The movement toward independence promises moral and spiritual regeneration. New structures must take the place of the colonial mechanism. The newly independent country must therefore seek to develop a whole array of instruments—a technology, so to speak, of change. Success will depend, however, upon the capacity to make use of all relevant experiences, past and present, domestic and external, as well as on the capacity for innovation.

We in the Caribbean have for some time been aware of the phenomenal nature of the obstacles in our path to nation building. Only now, however, are we becoming conscious of the richness of our experience and of our liberal human endowment. It is through this awareness that we shall overcome the obstacles.

On April 21, 1970—after this manuscript was virtually completed and following large-scale demonstrations arising from social unrest—the government of Trinidad and Tobago imposed a state of total emergency and became deadlocked in its relations with the army. Arms for the police were purchased from the United States against the very real possibility of the collapse of the government. As this preface was being written, nearly one hundred army personnel were being held on charges of mutiny, treason, and other offenses, and scores of civilians were either charged with sedition or put in prison under "preventive detention." The state of emergency was extended for seven months.

This book was intended to contribute to an understanding of the problems not only of Trinidad and Tobago and the Caribbean but also of ex-colonial countries in transition generally. I was especially concerned that my own country should avoid the deterioration leading to the "demonstration—state of emergency—army revolt" syndrome described in this work, a self-cycling condition that has made itself felt in many newly independent countries. If the inevitable gap of events between writing and publication has caused me some frustration, it has also added to the assurance with which I can present this study.

This work is the consequence of invitations extended to me to visit Harvard University, Boston College, and the Massachusetts Institute of Technology in the spring of 1968. There are many whose help I must acknowledge in making possible both the visit and the book: Dr. Robert Woetzel of Boston College, with whom I began a lasting friendship at Oxford University and whose encouragement has been forthcoming at every material stage; Mr. J. E. Leininger, Vice-Dean of Harvard Law School, who was kind enough to place the facilities of the Law School at my disposal, Professor Fritz Gustav Papanek, Director of the Harvard Development Advisory Service, with whom I had very useful discussions and who, in the midst of a very busy schedule, read and commented upon the early portions of the manuscript; Dr. Iqbal Gulatti, economic advisor in the Caribbean office of the Economic Commission for

Latin America (of the UN) and a former economic advisor to the government of Trinidad and Tobago; Mrs. Lynette Hutchinson for expert library assistance in the early stages; Mrs. Mavis Aqui for the painstaking work of typing the manuscript; and the many others who have shown a personal involvement in my labors. Finally, I thank my wife, Pat, and children, David and Ann-Margaret, who have borne my seclusions for the most part stoically, though sometimes rebelliously.

This is not an official book, nor must the persons I have mentioned here be associated with its views or its shortcomings. For these I am solely responsible.

A. N. R. Robinson
July 31, 1970

Colonialism – Spanish and British **1**

For most of our recorded history, Trinidad and Tobago have been under external control of one kind or another. Many of the problems that confront us today in our efforts toward transformation are directly traceable to colonial policies. To grasp the full effects of those policies, it is necessary to examine some of the conditions and events that brought them about.

Trinidad shows abundant evidence of permanent settlement by Caribs and Arawaks, and Tobago indicates at least periodic visits by Amerindian peoples long before Columbus arrived in 1498. His accounts show the gaily scarfed islanders he encountered in Trinidad to be similar to the other peoples with whom he had come in contact throughout the Caribbean. Few of these original inhabitants are left. As a consequence of colonization, slavery, and indenture, the population today is chiefly of African (43 percent) and East Indian (37 percent) descent, with a fair sprinkling of European, Chinese, and mixed ancestry.

During the 450 years following Columbus's discovery, Trinidad was under the sway of the Spanish and the British, while Tobago was the battleground for the French, the Dutch, the British, and occasional bands of touring pirates.

For the purpose of this work, only two of these periods will come under detailed examination—the Spanish and the British—as between them they share virtually the entire colonial era. Spain held its colony until the British took it by force in 1797. The Franco-British Treaty of Amiens in 1802 gave Britain formal possession of Trinidad. Tobago was to have gone to the French, but it remained in dispute until the French ceded it to Great Britain in the Treaty of Paris of 1814.

British rule was continuous from the beginning of the nineteenth century until 1962. Trinidad and Tobago joined in a Federation of the West Indies in 1958, and the United Kingdom maintained considerable influence, especially in financial affairs, until the federation collapsed and the country gained political independence on August 31, 1962.

It was not until 1888 that the two islands, just eighteen miles apart, were united to form one colony by an order-in-council of the United Kingdom; even then the union did not become fully effective until ten years later, again by an order-in-council. The order deemed Tobago a ward of the colony of Trinidad and Tobago; the term "ward" caused

THE SPANISH COLONIAL PERIOD 1

much misunderstanding in subsequent years.[1] Prior to the union, the islands had gone their divergent ways, exemplifying the absurd fragmentation that continues to be the outstanding political characteristic of the contemporary Caribbean landscape. Tobago was at one time administered with the Windward Islands, at another time with Barbados, and at still another time the island stood alone. Tobago has been the most disputed island in the Caribbean, and to this day it is still debated whether or not Columbus even really sighted the island and named it Bellafauna in 1498.

EARLY GOVERNORS

Columbus brought with him not only the science and technology of Europe but also Spanish policies on colonization, religion, and government. By the articles of agreement for his voyages, Columbus became admiral, viceroy, and governor-general of all the lands he discovered. He was also allowed to keep one-tenth of all gold, precious stones, and any other merchandise he acquired. Trinidad failed to offer precious metals but proved highly valuable as a stopping-off place during the long journey between Spain and the South American colonies.

Columbus died eight years after receiving the appointment, which his subsequent travels prevented him from carrying into effect. His son, Don Diego, who was allowed by an agreement with Spain to inherit his father's title in 1506, was interested in neither government nor development. His interests were gold and silver and precious stones.

In the document embodying his instructions, Ferdinand II demonstrated his solicitude for the native inhabitants, and on May 3, 1509, the king commanded the departing Diego:

You will say in my name to the Cacique and other principal Indians of said Island, that my will is that they and their Indians be well treated as our good subjects and nationals, and if hereafter anyone should do

1. An obvious error in the *Trinidad Royal Gazette* of December 8, 1898, has been perpetuated in all historical writing since the union with Trinidad. Whereas the instrument is described in Council Paper No. 177 as "The Secretary of State's Dispatch and Royal Order in Council Constituting Tobago a Ward of Trinidad," both the letter from the secretary of state, Joseph Chamberlain, and the actual terms of the order-in-council make it clear that Tobago was made a ward of the colony of Trinidad *and Tobago;* that is, for convenience the island was made an administrative area of the entire colony, and not an orphan or dependency of the larger island as it was commonly construed.

harm or evil they are to advise you of it, because you carry our orders to punish such cases very severely.[2]

At almost the first opportunity, however, Diego's men murdered 200 people, and Spain was outraged.

One of the more characteristic aspects of Spanish colonization, in the words of Rafael Altamira, was

the incessant struggle between, on the one hand, a State which was desirous of giving full protection to the Indian and was aided in this by all who shared the ideas which the legal norms expressed and, on the other hand, those greedy individuals who put their own private fortunes above everything else and sacrificed to personal pecuniary gain Indian liberties and Indian lives.[3]

The essence of the trouble was that the absolutist structure of Spanish government gave great latitude to such opportunists as Diego, both in public and private matters. Too much depended on the disposition and philosophical convictions of the individual. The abuse to which the system lent itself was further aggravated, again to use the words of Altamira, by the "divergence of opinion, which from the first was manifest among the men who influenced Spanish policy towards the Indians and which is reflected in official texts themselves, regarding the Indian's capacity to receive the civilization that Spain proffered him."[4]

In Trinidad, Diego failed in his appointed task of conquest and pacification and found no gold, to the displeasure both of himself and of Ferdinand II, who proceeded to withdraw Diego's commission and confer it on another Spaniard, Captain Roderigo de Bartidos. Diego, considering the appointment to be in violation of the agreement between the monarchy and his father, Columbus, threatened Bartidos with legal proceedings, thus causing Bartidos to desist from his claim.

Diego's death in 1526 presented Ferdinand with an opportunity to press conquest and pacification with greater vigor, and after royal reflection he selected, in 1530, Antonio Sedeño as the man to achieve his design. Sedeño was a man of some audacity; he had been imprisoned several times, and on one occasion set himself free by the ingenious device of burning down his prison. Unfortunately for both him and the

2. Eric Williams, *Documents of West Indian History, 1492-1655* (Trinidad: PNM Publishing, 1963), p. 189.
3. Rafael Altamira, *A History of Spain*, Muna Lee, trans. (Princeton, N.J.: Van Nostrand, 1949), p. 410.
4. *Ibid.*

king of Spain, Sedeño was destined for a life in prison, and in the course of his successful campaign of conquest and pacification of the indigenous inhabitants, he was again imprisoned, this time by a former subordinate.

The case of Sedeño dramatizes the nature and the hazards of the conquistador. Sedeño's mission remained unaccomplished, and it was not until 1570 that Spanish authority was firmly established by Juan Troche Ponce de León, whom Ferdinand rewarded with an appointment as governor and captain general.

Ponce de León held the appointment until 1591 when Antonio de Berrio replaced him. De Berrio was soon entangled in a jurisdictional dispute with the governor and captain general of Cumaná, who claimed Trinidad as one of his dependencies. The Council of the Indies, Spain's regional administrative apparatus, decided against de Berrio, but he, not unlike Diego, stuck tenaciously to his post.

De Berrio's career included capture by Sir Walter Raleigh in 1595 upon the latter's visit to Trinidad in search of El Dorado. However, de Berrio must have been inspired by his dealings with Sir Walter; after Raleigh's departure de Berrio, too, set out in search of El Dorado. The expedition finally broke him, though, and two years later he died.

Undeterred by his father's unsuccessful defense of his title, de Berrio's son, Ferdinand, seized control upon his father's death.

SPANISH ECONOMIC POLICY

Not long after the Spanish conquest, the indigenous Indians and Spanish immigrants in Trinidad began building up a prosperous but illegal trade with the English and Dutch, bartering tobacco for manufactured goods. This was in clear defiance of colonial trade policies, which prohibited a colony from trading not only with foreign countries and their colonies but even with other Spanish colonies. Ferdinand de Berrio, however, shut his eyes to the proceedings and took no action to suppress the trade. The Council of the Indies inquired into the affair, and as a result de Berrio was relieved of his governorship for five years.

Monopoly, Protection, and Regulation

The case of de Berrio illustrates the nature of the Spanish imperial trade pattern. Upon incorporation into the Spanish empire, Trinidad became part of the Spanish economic system. At the heart of the system were the principles of monopoly and the "exclusive"—the dominant features of not only Spanish but also all colonial economic organization.

Exclusivity in the case of Spain meant that the trade of every Spanish colony was confined to Spain, and Spain alone. Transport for the trade was organized in Spain and centralized at the port of Seville. Thereafter the ships sailed to and from the Indies by protected convoy. Given the condition of continual colonial wars and piracy, Spanish arms were essential to protect the commerce with the Indies.

Spain's principal economic interest in her colonies was gold. She was the first modern European country to become infatuated with the mercantilist theory and the first to suffer the disabling effects of the theory in practice. Monopoly, protection, and state regulation were the indispensable instruments by which the mercantile class could promote its own interest.[5]

The Spanish monarchy embraced the new economics without reservation, itself being the ultimate monopoly. No ship, no person, no thing was allowed to enter the Spanish Indies without express permission from the throne of Spain. Nothing left the Indies except by order of the governor. The privilege of mining for gold was granted only to those who were willing to settle and build homes in the colony. All gold so mined was melted and stamped, and the crown's share was delivered to the mayor, whose clerk made a proper record of the transaction.

By these and other means the Spanish monarchy accumulated the thousands of tons of gold that fed the appetite of the peculiar form of mercantilism known as "bullionism," which dominated economic thinking in Spain. However, a combination of the almost religious adherence to bullionist doctrine and the absence of a firm commercial base in which to invest led to hoarding and, far more serious, immoderate consumption, especially of luxury imports. So scanty a domestic productive capacity coupled with massive inflows of purchasing power created a textbook example of chronic inflation. Thus neither the colonies nor Spain benefited from the astronomical profits of the gold trade.

Economic Administration

The central administrative agency for the economic development of the

5. Eric Roll, *A History of Economic Thought* (London: Faber & Faber, 1953), p. 63.

colonies was the House of Trade, organized in 1503. It regulated all trade between Spain and the colonies, gathered economic and geographical data, and managed cartography. Under its supervision there evolved an elaborate and rigid commercial system, so powerful that Alonso Morgado describes it as "of the greatest moment of any in the world."[6] By the time of its abolition in 1790, it had irrevocably established the system of colonial monopoly. The basic principles underlying this system are the following:

1. The colonies existed for the strength, security, and wealth of the mother country.

2. They offered closed markets for Spanish manufacture and agriculture.

3. They supplied raw materials such as cotton, dyes, and hides and tropical luxuries such as sugar, cocoa, and tobacco.

4. They supplied the most desirable of all commodities, gold.

5. Trade and exploitation were organized on the basis of exclusivity or monopoly.

6. At the core of the economic system was the bullionist theory, which assumed that the most solid foundation of wealth was gold.

7. Colonial competition with the Spanish industry and agriculture was strictly forbidden.

In essence these principles became an economic example for all subsequent colonizing powers. Not only did Spain become the classic example of a modern power impoverished by gold; but she could not even meet the basic colonialist requirements of supplying her colonies with manpower, markets, and manufactured goods.

The inflation required policies to protect the consumer against rising prices, and these policies brought an already weak industrial and agricultural system into rapid decay. The system of the exclusive, never very effective, became thoroughly undermined as Spanish merchants were forced to look to foreign sources for capital and goods, and the colonies were forced to look for other markets.

Trinidad perfectly illustrates the dilemma of the colonies. Its principal commodity was tobacco, which, by the end of the sixteenth cen-

6. Veitia de Linaje, *Norte de la contraction de las Indias Occidentales* (Seville, 1672). English translation by John Stevens, *The Spanish Rule of Trade for the Indies* (London, 1702).

tury, the inhabitants were trading freely with the English and the Dutch for manufactured goods. So well did this trade prosper that the colonists were able to improve extensively the chief town of San Josef. However, because of a shortage of manpower, they turned to the Dutch and illicitly purchased 400 slaves to accomplish the task. De Berrio ignored the order from the Council of the Indies to stop the trade. Thereupon he was promptly suspended from his post for commercial, not humanitarian, reasons.

One of the few attempts Spain made to improve local conditions occurred near the end of its administration through the Cedula of Colonization of 1783. (See Appendix 1. The document itself is enlightening as to general Spanish colonial policy.) By this means Spain sought to ease the manpower shortage by opening the colony to non-Spanish immigrants. The move, coupled with financial incentives, produced a sizable influx of settlers, most of them from the neighboring French islands. It is from these settlers that Trinidad and Tobago derive the distinct Creole atmosphere so discernible today, the only significant non-British, European influence. It is somewhat ironical that Spain's most imaginative measure to keep the islands Spanish has survived with a decidedly French accent.

SPANISH COLONIAL ADMINISTRATION
Spain's highest authority for colonial administration was the Council of the Indies, which governed in the name of the crown. Its jurisdiction included all Spanish colonies in the New World as well as the Philippines.

The basic unit of government was the *gobernación*—provinces in the area originally granted to a discoverer for exploration and settlement—and subsequently the standard description applied to the area of control of a governor, earlier called an *adelantado* when he combined both civil and military functions. Several provinces were sometimes grouped together to form a captaincy general or viceroyalty. In addition to administrative areas, there were also judicial areas, *audiencias*, with limited administrative authority.

The Council of the Indies supervised the conduct of the governor. At the end of his term of office, he had to undergo a *residencia* or inquiry in the capital of the province, and all who wished were free to make complaints against the administration. After hearing the evidence, a commissioner appointed by the council decided how faithfully the governor had discharged his commission.

Another instrument of administration—one of more political than historical importance—was the *cabildo*. The jurisdiction of the *cabildo* was somewhat ill-defined, though it usually comprised the chief city of the colony and environs. Among its members were magistrates and other judicial officers, city and police officials, and members of prominent families in the area. Membership varied from a minimum of six to a maximum of twelve.

The main function of the *cabildo* was to act as a kind of watchdog over the rights of the citizenry. Its legal powers were severely limited, though some *cabildos* exercised considerable influence outside their jurisdictions, enough to be in constant conflict with the governors. In general, the *cabildo* was free to discuss all matters affecting the public welfare, and while it was essentially an advisory body, it did have some minor executive functions. In Trinidad, for example, the *cabildo* administered the oath of office to the colony's high officials and approved the qualifications of physicians, surgeons, and apothecaries. It granted licenses, inspected property, and collected rents; it paid the costs of the judiciary and the salaries of a physician and surgeon for the poor and a schoolmaster for the children of the poor.

The two fundamental weaknesses of the *cabildo* were the absence of any firm base of popular representation and the lack of adequate financial resources.[7] Where the right of election did exist, the governor could effectively annul this right by refusing to confirm the election. He could then fill the vacancies as he chose.

The *cabildo*, like most features of the Spanish colonial administration, later became subject to abuse, arising mainly from patronage and the sale of offices. The *cabildo* was nonetheless a significant innovation in Spanish administrative practice. By associating the inhabitants, however tenuously, with the government of the colony, it provided valuable experience in administration and offered an example of a forum for expressing local interests.

It was not merely incidental that the successor to the Trinidad *cabil-*

7. See John Lynch, *Spanish Colonial Administration, 1782-1810* (London: Athlone Press, 1958), pp. 205 ff.

do, the town council of Port-of-Spain under British administration, became the first representative institution in Trinidad, even though the franchise was restricted and its spirit of independence brought it into lengthy and violent conflict with the British secretary of state for the colonies. In a real sense, the *cabildo* in Trinidad, as in other places of Latin America, was an identifiable forerunner of the movement toward self-government.

Spanish administration continued until 1797, when the islands became caught up in the Napoleonic Wars. Trinidad fell to a British force of seventeen ships commanded by Rear Admiral Harvey and 8,000 men led by Sir Ralph Abercromby. Articles of capitulation were signed on February 18, 1797. The final change that the wars brought to the islands came in the Treaty of Paris of 1814, which placed Tobago, too, in the British fold.

While the British colonial period lasted only half the three centuries of Spanish rule, it is far more important historically, politically, and economically. Even today British influence in the country is considerable. The British legacy included legal and governmental systems and, of course, language.

The period is the lengthy forerunner and final jumping-off place to federation and independence. It was this period that witnessed the sowing of the seeds that would eventually grow into the massive political and economic problems the country has had to face in self-government.

BRITISH COLONIAL ADMINISTRATION

The Picton Era

The initial phase of British colonial administration in Trinidad was direct military rule, inaugurated under governor Thomas Picton, who was also commander in chief of the armed forces. Picton had arrived on the island with its captor, Sir Ralph Abercromby, in 1797 and officially assumed the governorship on June 29, 1801.

The law of the United Kingdom relating to conquered territories was clearly set out in the celebrated case of *Campbell* versus *Hall*[1] and embodied the following six propositions:

1. Conquered countries were to become dominions of the crown and subject to the laws of Parliament.
2. The inhabitants became British subjects and were not to be considered aliens.
3. The articles of capitulation and peace were to be inviolable according to their true intent and meaning.
4. Whoever settled in a conquered country became subject to local law and was to have no privileges distinct from the local inhabitants.
5. The laws of the country were to remain in force until altered by Parliament.
6. The king was barred from making changes contrary to fundamental principles, such as granting individual exemptions from trade laws or from the laws of Parliament.

In British terminology, the island became a crown colony. The governor in such a colony enjoyed considerable latitude in local administra-

1. Cowp. 204 (1774), Judgment of Lord Mansfield, C.J.

2 THE BRITISH COLONIAL PERIOD—NINETEENTH CENTURY

tion, but on matters of broad policy he was instructed by orders from the secretary of state for the colonies, through whom the governor reported to the British government, or by orders-in-council from the monarch's body of personal advisers, the Privy Council. The final and ultimate source of authority was, of course, the British Parliament.

Upon the appointment of Picton, the Trinidad *cabildo* petitioned its new sovereign, paying the usual deference to the crown and expressing "the universal joy and satisfaction of the inhabitants on learning that Trinidad is to become part of your Majesty's dominions." It asked for the continuation of Spanish law until a permanent form of government was worked out.

As there was no legislative council in Trinidad and Tobago, Picton had been instructed to appoint a council of advice, to consist of five prominent residents. The *cabildo,* on the other hand, proposed an assembly, elected from the eight districts in Port-of-Spain and the twenty-three parishes in the rest of the country, to recommend an administrative system most suited to Trinidad. It proposed that the assembly should also include two members of the governor's council of advice and that the governor should preside over it. Picton declined the suggestion because the English comprised only one-sixth of the population, and not even all of them were reliable. Picton's own proposal was to give temporary powers to handpicked planters and merchants.

The British government accepted neither proposal and until 1831 retained the council of advice. The council of advice was what its name implied, a purely advisory body, and Picton used it to whittle down what little influence the *cabildo* had retained.

Picton encountered many problems in his attempt to govern a citizenry of diverse racial origins and a large slave population. He opposed as unsuitable to Trinidad the normal crown colony government with a bicameral legislature. Moreover, he advocated the continuation of slavery at a time when it was clear that the system would soon be overthrown. A body of adventurers known as the "English Party" exploited his permission (under the convenience of existing Spanish law) to use torture on a young female witness. He also had poor relations with the Spanish population, only six or seven of whom he regarded as respectable. And he was unable to tolerate the "free people of color" of French descent, numbering over 3,000, whom he described in a dispatch to the secretary of state as "a dangerous class who must be gradually got rid of." "It is hoped," Picton continued, "that a great majority of them will emigrate on the giving up of the French islands. The adoption of proper measures will gradually reduce their numbers."[2]

In 1803, the British government, although affecting generally to endorse Picton's administration, had grave doubts about his ideas of orderly government and decided to replace the governor with a three-man commission consisting of a first commissioner, a naval commissioner, and Picton himself, whose title was changed to military commissioner. In his letter of appointment to the three commissioners, the British secretary of state said that the principal reason for appointing the commission was the need to reflect in the structure of government the diversity of the cultural origins of the island's inhabitants.

The year of the commissioners was a year of even more serious trouble for Trinidad. First Commissioner Colonel William Fullarton considered it his mission to discredit Picton, and the commission did more bickering than governing. The Privy Council eventually tried Picton for his role in the torture episode and found him guilty. He later obtained a retrial by the Court of King's Bench, however, which suspended the sentence. The court found that though the act was illegal, there was no malice, as torture was permitted in Trinidad under the Spanish law still in effect.

The system of government by commission produced utter confusion, and it was abolished within a year of its establishment; rule by the governor was restored.

Trinidad—an Exception to Democratization

In 1823 a royal commission of legal inquiry was appointed to determine the quality of the administration of civil and criminal justice in Trinidad. The commission reported, among other things, that it was "the unanimous feeling of all classes of the inhabitants that no change which did not at the same time confer on them the benefit of a reasonable control over the taxation and expenditure of the Colony, would be viewed by them as a boon from His Majesty's Government sufficient to satisfy their wants.[3] The eventual result of this report was the re-

2. Gertrude Carmichael, *History of the West Indian Islands of Trinidad and Tobago, 1498-1900* (London: Ridman, 1961), p. 53.
3. "Report of His Majesty's Commission of Legal Inquiry on the Colony of Trini-

placement, in 1831, of the council of advice with a council of government, Trinidad's first legislative body. It consisted of the governor, six officials, and six landowners. Introduced at the same time was a purely advisory executive council that included the colonial secretary, the attorney general, and the colonial treasurer, with the governor as president. There was, however, absolutely no concession to Trinidad in the matter of the democratic principles that had won almost universal acceptance in the Caribbean and had begun to cast light elsewhere in the British Empire.

The bicameral system following the British pattern of one elective and one nonelective chamber had, by 1763, become standard in all British colonies except Gibraltar, essentially a military base, and Minorca.

The unwillingness to allow any elective process in Trinidad stemmed first from the composition of the population and second from the fact that in other territories the elective chambers had already begun to serve as focal points of opposition to British governors.

The key to justifying the decision on Trinidad lay in the so-called "free people of color," the offspring of white planters and black slaves. On November 27, 1810, Lord Liverpool, the secretary of state for the colonies, wrote to the governor of Trinidad setting out the reasons for the exceptional treatment of the island:

First, if the free people of color, who were more numerous than whites, achieved equal rights, they would hold the power.

Second, a system that denied them equal rights might well subvert their loyalty.

Third, it was doubtful how consistent discriminatory treatment of the free people of color was with the spirit of the articles of capitulation, which guaranteed them the privileges they had enjoyed under the Spanish government.

Fourth, even the white population (French and Spanish) was largely ignorant of the British Constitution and unaccustomed to any form of government like it.

Fifth, to abolish the slave trade, the crown should retain its right of legislation and not subject itself to the embarrassments that would arise

dad, 29th June, 1827" (no. 551), Great Britain, *Parliamentary Papers* (Commons), 1826-1827, vol. 23, p. 883.

from any conflicts between Parliament and a subordinate legislature.[4]

Agitation continued for the creation of an elective assembly, however, and in a dispatch to the governor in 1832, Lord Groderich, secretary of state for the colonies, replied to a petition from a group of planters and merchants:

Theirs is a society in which the great mass of people to be governed are slaves, and their proposal is, that the laws should be made by a body composed of and elected by slave proprietors. Bringing their plan to the test of those general principles which I have already quoted in their own words, it is to be inquired how such a scheme would provide for that identity of interest which they rightly think ought to subsist between the legislator and the subject. . . . Society in Trinidad is divided into castes as strongly marked as those of Hindustan, nor can any man who has but an ordinary knowledge of the history and general character of mankind doubt what must be the effect of such distinction when in addition to their other privileges the superior race is entrusted with a legislative authority over the inferior.[5]

Lord Groderich obviously did not reject the idea of democracy or the principle of representation. In fact, in his dispatch to the governor on May 25, 1831, he had stated quite unequivocally, "The benefits resulting from the election by the proprietary body, in every country, of the popular branch of the legislature are too familiar to require notice, and are so universally admitted as to preclude all controversy on the abstract principle."[6]

Lord Groderich's sentiments notwithstanding, Trinidad, which had been the exception, was soon to become the rule. During the course of the century, the Trinidad pattern was repeated throughout the British Caribbean, except for the Bahamas, Bermuda, and Barbados. The new system in the other territories of the Caribbean reflected the decline of the power of the planter class that resulted from the growth of competition in the world sugar industry and the abolition of slave labor. Abolition in 1834 brought legal equality to former slaves, but political equality was a century beyond and more.

THE VALUE OF THE CARIBBEAN COLONIES TO BRITAIN
There is no need to detail the elements that made up British colonial

4. Hewon Craig, *The Legislative Council of Trinidad and Tobago* (London: Faber & Faber, 1952), p. 19.
5. *Ibid.*
6. *Ibid.*, p. 18.

economics, as they were essentially like those of Spain, indeed of all the major European colonial powers. True, Britain relied less heavily on monopoly, but the "exclusive" retained its importance.

It will be useful, however, to note briefly just why the Caribbean islands, known then as the Sugar Islands, were so attractive to colonialists. Some notion of the value attached to Caribbean colonies in the eighteenth century can be gained from the fact that following the Seven Years' War, there was considerable debate over whether Britain should demand from France the island of Guadaloupe or Canada.

The value of the British Caribbean colonies in the seventeenth and eighteenth centuries is documented by Dr. Eric Williams in *Capitalism and Slavery*.[7] In 1697 Barbados alone, with 166 square miles of land, was worth more in terms of the value of imports to Britain than New England, New York, and Pennsylvania combined. In 1773 British exports to Jamaica were 30 percent greater than those to New York and Pennsylvania combined. Over the period 1714-1773 British imports from Montserrat (33 square miles) were triple the value of those from Pennsylvania; those from Nevis (50 square miles) were double those from New York; those from Antigua (108 square miles) were triple those from New England; those from Barbados were double those from the "bread colonies" of New England, New York, and Pennsylvania combined. As an export market for the same years, Jamaica was as valuable as New England. Barbados and Antigua together were as good a market as New York, and Montserrat and Nevis better than Pennsylvania.

No tribute to the value of the West Indian colonies to Great Britain could exceed the one by Sir Winston Churchill in 1938, when he said:

Our possession of the West Indies, like that of India . . . , gave us the strength, the support, but especially the capital, the wealth, at a time when no other European nation possessed such a reserve, which enabled us to come through the great struggles of the Napoleonic wars, the keen competition of commerce in the eighteenth and nineteenth centuries, and enabled us not only to acquire the appendage of possessions which we have, but also to lay the foundations of that commercial and financial leadership which, when the world was young, when everything out-

7. Eric Williams, *Capitalism and Slavery* (London: André Deutsch, 1964), pp. 54-55.

side Europe was undeveloped, enabled us to make our great position in the world."[8]

Currency Control

In fact, by the 1820s the area had grown so important financially that currency control became necessary. In the seventeenth century, sugar and cotton had been used as money throughout the Caribbean. They circulated in Trinidad alongside the silver and gold coins of Portugal and Spain and were in use in all the territories—British, French, and Spanish.

In 1825, by a means of treasury minute, the British put an end to the confused state of affairs. The purpose of the treasury minute was "to introduce a fixed and uniform medium of exchange of all transactions connected with the Public Service in place of the various fluctuating and anomalous currencies which have been created under the pressure of temporary emergencies or with the view to local and peculiar emergencies." Also, the British government wanted a uniform currency with which to pay its troops. In the words of Robert Chalmers, in his *History of Currency in the British Colonies*, "the intention of the Treasury minute of 1825 was that the shilling should circulate wherever the British drum was heard."[9]

Notes were not in circulation as early as 1825, but it was a British bank, Barclays, that first made use of them. Barclays was then called the Colonial Bank; later it became the British, Dominion, Colonial, and Overseas Bank. Following came three Canadian banks: the Royal Bank of Canada, the Canadian Imperial Bank of Commerce, and the Bank of Nova Scotia. It was not until 1906 that the colonial government of Trinidad and Tobago began issuing notes.

Social Effects

One system of great value to Britain was that of the plantation, which produced cotton for her textile mills and molasses for her sugar factories. It was also, however, a system based on African slave labor, which resulted in a society culturally barren and plagued with the evils of col-

8. Quoted in Eric Williams, *The Negro in the Caribbean* (Washington, D.C.: Associates in Negro Folk Education, 1942), p. 18.
9. Quotations from the Treasury Minute and from Robert Chalmers (London: 1893) are found in H. A. de S. Gunasekera, *From Dependent Currency to Central Banking in Ceylon* (London: G. Bell, 1962), p. 9.

or prejudice. With the end of the Napoleonic Wars came parliamentary abolition of the slave system in the British colonies. In Trinidad and Tobago and Guiana, however, a different sort of slave system took its place: indentured East Indian "contract labor" was imported to replace the Africans who on emancipation refused to continue to work in the plantations.

Where minerals were discovered, as in Trinidad, Jamaica, and Guiana in the early part of the nineteenth century, local operations were limited to extraction; refining and manufacturing took place outside of the area. Thus the power of the colonial mercantile class continued to grow.

Public education was virtually nonexistent, and it was left to the Christian missionaries to do the little they could. The few who could afford it sent their children to schools in Great Britain. The system was only slightly mitigated by a moderate tolerance of the free people of color, the result of miscegenation between planter and slave.

For Trinidad—whose size and diversification, however limited, gave it a certain amount of stamina to recover from temporary reversals—the system was harsh and unresponsive only to the native inhabitants. For tiny Tobago, however, the system allowed no recuperative powers, and when trouble came, its product was not hard times but utter collapse.

FACTORS LEADING TO UNION

No island in the Caribbean has had a more tortuous history than Tobago. Yet as late as 1862 the island rivaled St. Kitts for first place in sugar production in the West Indies. Statistics for the early nineteenth century disclose that in 1839, whereas imports were £113,371, exports amounted to £183,566, a trade surplus of over £70,000.[10] The 1957 Tobago Development Team reported that "Had the necessary capital, labour and skill been available in the 19th century, when things began to decline, the island might well have been one of the most prosperous territories in the Caribbean. . . ."[11]

The difference between the experience of Tobago and those of many other West Indian islands is one of degree, not kind. Mining and agricul-

10. *Tobago, Planning Team Report* (Trinidad: Colonial Development and Welfare, 1957), p. 20.
11. *Ibid.*

ture did not provide the diversification necessary for it to withstand even the more common hazards of such an economy. If Trinidad is a vivid example of the failure of Spain's colonial economic system, Tobago offers an illustration of the failure of Britain's.

The union of the two islands in 1888 was the final admission of the failure of both separatism and the one-crop economy. The British had considered integrating the Caribbean colonies from time to time and had even attempted it to a limited degree and in specific areas, but their purpose in uniting the islands always centered on reducing administrative costs rather than promoting economic development. It is true that conditions in the Caribbean were chaotic because of the military operations of the imperial powers, and this fact militated against an effective policy of unification; however, no such policy even existed, and until very recent times no attempts at unification were made.

The immediate cause of the union of 1888 arose from the collapse of the Tobago economy. The policy of limiting colonial economic development to supplying luxury goods and raw materials led to the system of one-crop economies in the Caribbean, the principal crops being sugar and cotton. As long as demand remained strong, the supply continued to expand. As long as prices were high, income was buoyant and consumption high. However, the government's tax base was narrow, and there was no policy of saving and capital accumulation, no policy of reinvestment, no development planning, and no long-range economic projections. The premise of the system was that what was good for the mother country was good enough for the colonies, a notion that survives today in a new guise and sometimes forms the basis of relations between the rich countries and the less developed.

For Tobago the system was at its least debilitating in the eighteenth century, when comparative peace prevailed. Demand for sugar in Britain was strong. The revolution and its aftermath had created unsettled conditions in the French possessions, thereby reducing competition, and the British navy was supreme. The price of sugar nearly tripled between 1793 and 1798. However, savings were unknown in government operations and policies, and what revenues there were quickly became expenditures.

Enforced economic improvidence could hardly lead to any consequence but financial irresponsibility. To colonial officers in metropolitan countries, local governments did not exist to manage or oversee the economy, least of all to provide for the future. Their business was to preserve order and hold the stirrup for private enterprise. When they entered the commercial arena, it was only to ensure that private enterprise kept the imperial rules.

According to A. R. Prest,

The administration itself was essentially conducted in the intelligent amateur tradition—there was a natural abhorrence for the mysteries of such obscure and mystifying subjects as economics. In as far as advice was sought outside the Government, it was mainly taken from the men of established position in trade and commerce, whose natural instinct was to keep government expenditure (and hence taxation) at a minimum and at all costs to ensure that there was no encroachment on their traditional preserves.[12]

The sugar industry in Trinidad and Tobago began running into difficulties after the abolition of slavery in 1833. The industry lost its supply of cheap labor and had to seek new sources. The planters were compensated, but the slaves were not. From 1844, East Indian indentured immigrants began to replace the African slaves. However, toward the middle of the century, the industry again began to fare badly, this time because of competition from Cuba, for example, where sugar production was on a much larger scale and technologically more advanced, and also from Europe, where beet sugar production had been increasing since Napoleon instituted the Continental System as a counterforce to the British blockade. By the 1870s the sugar industry was bankrupt in Tobago, and not long afterward it was on the verge of collapse in Trinidad.

The local management of Tobago's plantation economy was in the hands of planters. Their vested interest was sugar. Their economy was of the one-crop variety. Their territory was a small island of a few thousand souls. Ultimate responsibility for its destiny lay with the imperial power. It is not surprising that the philosophy of laissez-faire expressed itself in the social attitude of eat, drink, and be merry.

In a memorandum to the secretary of state for the colonies dated November 1, 1875, Augustus Gore, the governor of Tobago, observed quite candidly that there was no need for Tobago to maintain a separate government from that of Trinidad. "The distance from Trinidad to

12. A. R. Prest, *A Fiscal Survey of the British Caribbean* (London: HMSO, 1957), pp. 8-9.

Tobago is only 18 miles from land to land, and if a good road was made from Port-of-Spain to Toco, and a steam launch was employed, daily communications might be established between Port-of-Spain and Scarborough."[13]

One of the reasons for Gore's conclusion was "the small amount of work done by the officials," whose salaries he declared his intention to abolish. Gore continued, "I am aware that, in making these proposals, I am, so to speak, cutting my own throat, but I have no fear that if I do my duty on this, calling attention to the saving that could be expected, Her Majesty's Government will not make me suffer."[14]

In 1883 the British government appointed a commission of inquiry to make recommendations for the improvement of the economic structure of Grenada, St. Vincent, St. Lucia, and Tobago. The commission supported Gore's proposal, and Parliament empowered Queen Victoria to declare the union by an order-in-council.

Not until much later did it become clear that the economic problems of Tobago as well as of all the Caribbean islands were insoluble within a context of separatism and one-crop economies and that the essence of economic growth was integration and diversification. What was needed was an integration based on equality and animated by the philosophy of the greatest good for the greatest number. Such an economic system, supported by a similarly directed political system, is the only enduring arrangement for economic and political union. This sort of arrangement, though, was still far in the future.

UNION
Under the authority of Parliament, Trinidad and Tobago were united by an order-in-council November 17, 1888; the order took effect the following January 11.

The order-in-council, however, was really only the precursor of complete union, which did not occur until 1898. In view of the barriers that have grown up in the path to Caribbean unity in the twentieth century and the concomitant emergence of mini- and microstates, it may be enlightening to examine the articles of union. The order-in-council was a

13. C. R. Ottley, *Complete History of the Island of Tobago in the West Indies* (Trinidad: Guardian Commercial Printery, n.d.), p. 66.
14. *Ibid.*

complicated instrument carefully designed to take into account the differences in the political, constitutional, and financial conditions of the two islands. The main provisions were as follows:

1. As of January 11 the authority of the governor of the Windward Islands over Tobago was abrogated, and the executive and legislative councils of Tobago were abolished. In place of them, there was established a commissioner and a financial board consisting of two appointed and three *elected* members.

2. The authority of the governor of Trinidad was extended to include all of the new colony of Trinidad and Tobago.

3. The commissioner was given all the authority of the governor of Trinidad and Tobago except the power to appoint and suspend public officials and the power of executive clemency.

4. The commissioner was an ex-officio member of the legislative council of Trinidad and Tobago.

5. The commissioner and at least one elected member of the financial board were to be residents of Tobago.

The elected members of the financial board in Tobago were elected on a fairly broad franchise, the only property qualification being the payment of no less than ten shillings in direct taxes or rates during the year preceding the election.

The financial board's regulations had the force of law, subject to assent by the governor and the queen. Any member of the board could move any resolution, introduce any regulation, or propose any question for debate, though revenue resolutions required the consent of the governor of Trinidad and Tobago before they could be introduced.

An unusual though understandable provision dealing with Tobago was Article 27, which restrained the legislature of Trinidad and Tobago from altering taxes or duties in Tobago except customs duties, duties on shipping, and excise duties on rum and other spirits; the article also disallowed appropriation of any part of the revenues raised in Tobago for anything except the public services of Tobago. In all other matters, in case of conflicting laws or regulations, those of the legislature were to prevail over those of the financial board.

To reinforce its financial provisions, the order-in-council decreed that the revenues, expenditures, and debts of Tobago be kept distinct from those of Trinidad. Subsidiary provisions forbade any customs barriers between the two islands and declared that customs duties collected in Trinidad on imports eventually consumed in Tobago were to be considered Tobago revenue, and vice versa.

The order-in-council of 1888 remained in effect until the order-in-council of November 1, 1898, which merged the revenues, expenditures, and debts of Tobago with those of the united colony. Variations between Trinidad and Tobago in the levels of a number of taxes remained.[15]

Neither island wanted unitary statehood, but feelings ran much higher in Tobago. While Trinidad feared that the effect would be merely to transfer the burdens of Tobago from the United Kingdom to herself, Tobago feared subservience to Trinidad.

Although the legislative council of Tobago accepted unitary statehood, it put its reservation on record in the following resolution:

That inasmuch as the wish of the people of Tobago for union with Trinidad has principally been based on the representations of the government, and the assurance given to the people that material benefit will result to Tobago from that union, the Secretary of State for the Colonies be respectfully asked in the event of such union taking place, to afford the people of Tobago a pledge, that should it prove disadvantageous to the colony, or otherwise undesirable to the majority of its inhabitants, this colony shall on petition have granted back to it the form of self-government which now exists here.[16]

A sensible and obvious step thus gave rise to misgivings that proved not altogether unjustifiable, as the history of the union demonstrated. What was to have been a union of equality degenerated into one of patent inequality, one of the superior and the inferior, one of territory and dependency, and Trinidad's feelings seeped into both official and unofficial attitudes toward the smaller island. The nadir of Tobago's decline was its complete elimination from the political map of the Caribbean; citations in official documents and elsewhere referred to Trinidad only, on the assumption that Tobago was simply a part of Trinidad.

THE END OF THE CENTURY

Metropolitan Reassertion
While the distances between the islands of the Caribbean are to this day

15. See Appendix 2.
16. Ottley, *History of Tobago*, p. 69.

cited as an argument against union, this same argument was largely discounted in the nineteenth century. The chief obstacle neither was nor is distance; the difficulty lies in overcoming the sense of isolation and separation that the imperial system so effectively had instilled. Europe was the center of the Caribbean in administration, in communication, and in education. Inhabitants of all the territories knew less about one another than they knew about Europe.

In 1884 L. A. A. de Verteuil, a Trinidadian, wrote:

So foreign and remote are the relations existing between the different colonies that the inhabitants of Trinidad are better acquainted with events in Europe, and even in China, than those in Jamaica and the Bahamas. Again, so diversified and dissimilar are their laws in general, and the regulations of their courts of justice in particular, that a barrister of good repute in Trinidad would be obliged to undergo a fresh training before practising in the neighbouring colony of Grenada. And yet the interests of these different islands are nearly identical. They must rise or fall together. It is, therefore, highly essential that these different dependencies should be homogenized, as far as possible—that they should be brought into mutual relations and contact, so that the least advanced may profit by the experience of those that are more precocious—that their natural resources should become known, and their individual wrongs be felt and acknowledged as the wrongs of all; thus, and thus only, will they be able to afford each other aid and support in difficulties and distress. This, however, can be done only by forming a political union of the scattered colonies.[17]

Long before this, the absurdity of the entire Caribbean situation was highlighted by H. Merivale, an official of the colonial office, in a lecture to Oxford University. Merivale's observations were both penetrating and scathing:

Each little community, of a few thousand souls only, has its miniature king, lords and commons, its governor, council, and assembly, together with a host of administrative and paid functionaries, most disproportioned to its importance. And each assembly guards (or until very recently guarded) with the utmost jealousy, not only the right of taxation, but the anarchical prerogative of voting away at will, without any initiative proposal by the governor. All this overweighted system of local government is a relic of times past away. So long as England continued tributary to these islands, by the monopoly which she accorded to their sugar, she requited herself, to some extent, by maintaining in the West Indies places for English functionaries and sinecurists paid by West Indian money. The system has ceased; but many of the places remain; and the impoverished communities, which can scarcely afford to

17. L. A. A. de Verteuil, *Trinidad* (London: Cassell, 1884), p. 29.

pay the salaries, seem, nevertheless, to entertain the strongest objection to reducing or consolidating offices which have become objects of local ambition.[18]

Merivale went on to suggest,

Whatever slight reason there may have been in former days for the maintenance of these small local governments has been wholly taken away by [the] modern facility of communication. They should be united, and this rather by consolidation than federation.[19]

What Merivale was proposing was not only centralization but, more importantly, the transfer of power from local elected legislatures to the governor, an official of the imperial government. This is precisely what did take place, but not for the purpose of consolidation or federation. By the end of the nineteenth century, every West Indian territory except Barbados had lost its representative assembly.

The transfer of power to the Colonial Office reflected the decline in strength of local proprietary interests, and it was the intention of the British government to reassert control. The golden opportunity for unification that then presented itself passed, and the old parochialisms reasserted themselves in the mixed assemblies of elected and appointed members that replaced the bicameral legislatures. These parochialisms were intensified with every devolution of authority to the hands of local representatives. Thus there were variations in currency, trade legislation, taxation, and constitutional development.

This does not mean that the whole idea of unification had been thrown into limbo. It was pursued halfheartedly at times toward federalism, at other times toward unitary statehood, but seldom with vigor and never with metropolitan encouragement.

A Moment of Unity

Trinidad and Tobago closed the fourth and final full century of colonial rule not with a whimper but a bang. And although the report from it failed to produce lasting reverberations, it demonstrated clearly that the piece that fired the round was serviceable for further action.

By an ordinance of June 1, 1840, the *cabildo*, then known as "the Illustrious Cabildo," was replaced by a town council in Port-of-Spain. The town council comprised the governor, as president ex-officio, and

18. H. Merivale, *Lectures on Colonization and Colonies, Delivered before the University of Oxford in 1839, 1840, and 1841* (Oxford: Oxford University Press, 1928), p. 1347.
19. *Ibid.*

twelve councillors, who served a single three-year term. The voting requirements were a minimum age of twenty-one, residence within three miles of Port-of-Spain, and either one year's occupancy in a house taxable at a minimum of $200 or payment of annual rent of at least $200. Finally, the council elected its chairman from its membership. Thus the Port-of-Spain town council was, from its establishment, a representative institution.

Not long after 1840, however, difficulties arose between the council and the central government, which continually encroached on the council's revenue-earning preserves. The council often found itself with deficits and resorted to borrowing and selling its properties; in 1896 it sold the town hall to the central government for £5,000.

A political event of major significance in the history of the country occurred in 1898 when secretary of state for the colonies Joseph Chamberlain, after a two-year struggle, abolished the town council.

Chamberlain had developed a strong determination to bring municipal bodies under his control. Among the conditions he laid down for financial assistance from the central government, Chamberlain instructed that the governor approve the budget of the town council prior to its becoming effective. The council took this as an affront to the oldest representative institution in the country and rejected Chamberlain's instruction out of hand. Chamberlain threatened to abolish the council if it did not heed him. The council dared the colonial secretary to carry out his threat, which he did. Upon abolition, the administration of the town was handed over to the town commissioner until the council's restoration in 1914.

The council's stand was a popular one, and its last act before abolition was a demonstration, led by the mayor, through the streets of Port-of-Spain to the cheers of the citizenry. To them, the act of defiance was more important than the loss of the council. This was the first significant manifestation of a developing spirit of nationalism in Trinidad. The people were not successful, but the people were together.

THE EFFECTS OF UNION

With the discovery of petroleum resources in Trinidad at the beginning of the twentieth century, the island rapidly became the most prosperous in the British Caribbean. However, as Trinidad was gaining a reputation for its prosperity, Tobago was becoming notorious for its poverty. Trinidad's crude oil production increased from 125,112 barrels in 1910 to 2,083,027 barrels in 1920, but agricultural production in Tobago made no significant progress. Both internal and external communications steadily deteriorated. In the West Indies Tobago had become a byword for neglect.

A natural consequence was migration from Tobago to Trinidad, a fact clearly revealed in the vital statistics for the period 1901-1946. Over the decade 1901 to 1911, the population of Tobago increased by 2,000; over the succeeding decade, there was an increment of 2,640. But from 1921 to 1930, the population increase was only 1,970, and between 1931 and 1946 there was an overall growth of just 1,840. This trend occurred in spite of the fact that the infant mortality rate in Tobago had been consistently lower than the average for the country as a whole. By 1946 Tobago had become, in relation to arable land, among the most underpopulated islands in the British Caribbean. Of all these territories, only British Honduras was less densely populated than Tobago. (See Table 3.1.)

The pattern appeared everywhere—neglect of roads, of basic services such as water and fuel, of agriculture, and of the island's tourist potential. The government made no provision for education above the primary school level, despite the absence of any contact with the outside world except through Trinidad.

If this was what political, economic, or any other kind of union meant, it is hardly surprising that no other island wanted any part of it. It is significant that when the federation came into being, Montserrat with 32 square miles (as against Tobago's 116 square miles) and 13,000 people (as against Tobago's 35,000) entered as a separate unit with representation in its own right in the West Indian Federal Parliament.[1]

---

1. Ten seats were allocated to Trinidad and Tobago. However, Tobago's population of 35,000, compared with Trinidad's of 600,000, gave no assurance that Tobago would have its own representative.

3 THE BRITISH COLONIAL PERIOD—TWENTIETH CENTURY

Table 3.1. Population in Relation to Arable Land in British Caribbean Territories, 1946

Territory	Acres of Arable Land Excluding Pastureland	Total Population (to nearest hundred)	Number of Persons per Acre of Arable Land
Barbados	61,200	227,600	3.7
British Guiana	280,000	460,000	1.6
British Honduras	1,336,000	78,100	0.06
Jamaica	694,200	1,517,700	2.2
Antigua (including Barbuda)	23,400	50,900	2.2
Montserrat	9,500	14,100	1.5
St. Kitts-Nevis-Anguilla	28,300	55,600	1.9
Virgin Islands	5,500	7,600	1.4
Trinidad	315,000	664,300	2.1
Dominica	49,700	59,000	1.2
St. Lucia	32,100	86,200	2.7
St. Vincent	30,700	75,200	2.4
Grenada	51,000	85,300	1.7
Tobago	39,100	33,300	0.85

Source: *Tobago Planning Team Report* (Trinidad: Colonial Development and Welfare, 1957), Table 3, p. 30.

Therefore the agony of Anguilla's secessionist movement and of Barbuda's recently advocated separatism is understandable in a historical context. When it came to sharing burdens, the classic United Kingdom policy toward the West Indies had been to treat West Indians as though they were all alike. It was natural for West Indians to resent this approach and to suspect any British move toward any kind of union as a possible attempt to escape its responsibilities for the poorer islands by transferring them to the more prosperous ones.

The feeling has survived in the form of suspicion toward recent suggestions for Caribbean union. It should be noted that Tobago's difficulties are considerably less severe than in the past, but many problems remain. It may well be that before Trinidad and Tobago can convince others of the wisdom of union, we will have to present a better example of our own union.

Aside from minor reforms, there were few advancements in the turmoil before and during World War I. Afterward, though, the upheavals emanating from the war and growing dissatisfaction with economic and political conditions led to increasing social and political ferment. As a consequence, the British government dispatched Sir Thomas Wood to the Caribbean in 1922 to formulate proposals for reform. The Wood Report and the resulting Constitution of 1924 represent major landmarks in the political development of Trinidad and Tobago.

In 1922, on the occasion of his visit to the Caribbean and British Guiana, Wood emphasized the weakness in the West Indian situation:

The ordinary student of politics sees a large number of British Colonies, all situated in the same part of the world, faced with very similar economic and political problems, each maintaining a separate government supported by a separate revenue, each trying to work out its destiny alone and unassisted, at a time when the whole tendency both in the British Empire and in the world at large is in the direction of bringing together such small and scattered fragments into large units.[2]

Wood cited one telling example of the inability of the territories to carry their weight in the affairs of the empire: the experience of the Canadian government in having to arrange mutual preference with ten separate West Indian governments. "It is obvious," he said, "that such a situation cannot be best calculated to promote common policy and common action."[3]

The first and most serious obstacle to more concerted action, according to Wood, was physical. The distance between Jamaica and the nearest British islands was almost 1,000 miles, and the journey from Jamaica to the Lesser Antilles and British Guiana took longer than the journey to the United Kingdom. Aggravating the physical problem was the lack of direct communication. Mail from Jamaica to Trinidad, Barbados and British Guiana went via London, New York, or Halifax. There was a great practical difficulty of communication even within the existing federations of the Leeward Islands and the Windward Islands.

The supreme obstacle, however, was the colonial pattern of trade employed by all imperial powers. Said Wood: "The colonies are bound to

2. E. F. L. Wood, M.P., *Report on His Visit to the West Indies and British Guiana, December 1921 to February 1922*, Cond. 1679 (Great Britain Colonial Office, 1922), p. 29. Hereafter, Wood Report.
3. *Ibid.*

export their produce almost entirely to Europe or North America and to import for their requirements from the same sources. There is, consequently, no volume of intercolonial trade to support the kind of intercolonial service that would, for political reasons, be desirable."[4] There was no communication because there was no trade, and there could be no trade without altering the imperial pattern.

Another difficulty that Wood mentioned was political diversity, the very thing the crown colony system was designed to eliminate. Wood proposed associating the Windward Islands with Trinidad, with the proviso that "it must be made clear that an essential condition of approval by the Secretary of State will be a deliberate opinion in favour of the change in the Colonies themselves."[5]

Wood did not recommend granting self-government, which was being introduced in a number of colonies in the early twentieth century. He based his decision on four factors he found present in Trinidad: (1) the mixed character of the population, (2) the absence of "a learned class," (3) the need for uniformity of administration with the adjacent colonies, and (4) the restricted nature of the franchise.

Wood actually recommended little more than a concession to the principle of representation. He proposed seven elected members out of a total of twenty-five members including twelve officials. He proposed no change in the executive council, whose composition was to remain purely official and whose functions were to be purely advisory.[6] It was not an earthshaking event; it was not even a bold reform. Nevertheless, once representation had become a right in practice, democracy had breached the conservative stronghold. Thereafter, conditions changed more in four decades than they had in four centuries. In point of fact, the Wood constitution was obsolete before it was committed to paper. Democratic pressures for reform continued to build with growing social unrest in Trinidad and Tobago and in the whole of the Caribbean.

Among others presenting a case for reform was the president of the Workingman's Association, Captain Arthur Andrew Cipriani, who subsequently assumed an eminent role in the political life of the country.

For years Cipriani and others sought to bring changes, but with little

4. *Ibid.*, p. 30.
5. *Ibid.*, p. 33.
6. *Ibid.*

success. Then in 1935 a reform movement sprang up around Uriah Butler, a bearded, freewheeling agitator of considerable, though uneven, talent. The movement was handicapped, unfortunately, by its leader's limited education and the lack of a concrete program. However, it held together long enough so that by 1937 the general discontent in Trinidad and Tobago and throughout the Caribbean territories had led to the appointment of another royal commission of inquiry, under the chairmanship of Lord Moyne, to study the conditions throughout the West Indies. Two of the commission's most significant findings were, first, that the West Indian discontent was symptomatic of social and economic ills that could be remedied only by a general rehabilitation of West Indian society and, second, that the demand of the people for a larger voice in the management of their affairs was genuine and reflected widespread and growing political consciousness.[7]

The Moyne Report rejected the policy of laissez-faire and the policy of slow political progress toward majority rule; instead, it called for more vigorous representation by the people in formulating official policies.

As a consequence of the Moyne Report, nominated members of the legislative council were removed in 1940, and the elected members were increased commensurately from seven to nine. The most significant change, however, was in the composition of the executive council in 1941, which for the first time embodied an elected majority.

THE BASE AT CHAGUARAMAS
Another matter of lasting importance for Trinidad and Tobago occurred in 1941 when the United States gave Britain fifty overage destroyers in exchange for ninety-nine-year leases on eight bases stretching from Canada to South America, among them the Chaguaramas base in Trinidad. The 1941 agreement was the culmination of discussions that began more than a year before in an exchange of notes between the United States secretary of state, Cordell Hull, and the British ambassador, the Marquis of Lothian. The bases were located in Newfoundland, Bermuda, the Bahamas, Jamaica, Antigua, St. Lucia, British Guiana, and, of course, Trinidad and Tobago. At that time the

7. Lord Moyne, *West India Royal Commission Report*, Cmd. 6607 (London: HMSO, 1945).

United Kingdom was so desperate that it would have been quite willing to go so far as to cede complete sovereignty over the islands to the United States. Roosevelt considered that he could adequately secure United States interests by using the bases without taking complete responsibility for the islands' affairs. As he so trenchantly put it, "If we can get our naval bases, why, for example, should we buy with them two million headaches, consisting of that number of human beings who would be a definite drag on this country, and who would stir up questions of racial stocks by virtue of their new status as American citizens?"[8]

The U.S. government sought maximum benefit with minimum responsibility. The extent of power it obtained was unprecedented in British colonial history. The U.S. ambassador in London, John G. Winant commented:

I think it contains everything we need to use these bases effectively. The rights and powers it conveys are far-reaching, probably more far-reaching than any the British Government has ever given anyone over British territory before. They are not used to giving such concessions and on certain points they have fought every inch of the way. While they have intended all along to give us everything we really needed—they could do no less and had no desire to do less—it was a real struggle for them to break habits of 300 years. The Prime Minister has been generous throughout. Certain powers, notably those in Article XII, are so sweeping that the British would never have granted them except as a natural consequence of the original agreement and the spirit which it embodies.[9]

The article referred to allowed the United States unrestricted and tax-free use of the island's roads.

Article VI, however, was far more sweeping:

Special Emergency Powers
When the United States is engaged in war or in time of other emergency, the Government of the United Kingdom agree that the United States may exercise in the Territories and surrounding waters or air spaces all such rights, power and authority as may be necessary for conducting any military operations deemed desirable by the United States, but these rights will be exercised with all possible regard to the spirit of the fourth clause of the Preamble.[10]

8. Letter to the secretary of state, Cordell Hull, dated January 11, 1941. *Foreign Relations of the United States, 1941*, vol. 3 (Washington: U.S. Government Printing Office, 1959), p. 3.
9. *Foreign Relations of the United States, 1941*, p. 84.
10. The fourth clause of the preamble expressed the desire that the agreement "shall be fulfilled in a spirit of good neighbourliness between the Government of

Clearly the provisions did not contemplate so fundamental a change as the movement toward independence that took place after the Second World War. In Trinidad and Tobago there were objections not only to the nature of the provisions but also to the manner of their application.

British governor Sir Hubert Young persistently pursued these objections on behalf of the local inhabitants, as there was no elected assembly at the time. Young proved to be an unrelenting champion of Trinidad and Tobago's interests, voicing vigorous opposition especially to the choice and number of areas the American military authorities selected. He pointed out that the main area, the Northwest Peninsula, was Port-of-Spain's natural area of expansion and that it was one of the country's finest natural recreational centers. He further argued that having bases in the northwest, the center, and other areas would inevitably involve the military in the life of the country, that it would disrupt national development, and finally that it would deprive the population of much needed space. He proposed instead the reclamation of a large swamp area for the base, thus adding to the country's resources and eliminating the possibility of continuing grievance. He also foresaw the lease conflicting with the country's aspirations to self-government. This, however, was a long-range view and carried little weight in those desperate times.

In any case, the agreement became fact, and the population began to experience the more positive effects of the military presence. It should be noted that, disagreements on details notwithstanding, the country felt this was its loyal contribution not only to the mother country but also to the defense of freedom. United States money was extremely beneficial, especially during the construction phase. The relationship between American military and local civilian population came to be immortalized in the popular calypso, which begins gaily with "Drinking rum and Coca-Cola" and ends pointedly with "Mother and daughter both working for the Yankee dollar."

Chaguaramas caused its share of difficulties in the war years, but no one at the time dreamed it could become so volatile an issue as to play a central role in the collapse of the Federation of the West Indies.

---

the United Kingdom and the Government of the United States of America, and that details of its practical application shall be arranged by friendly co-operation.

The Sterling Area

After the Second World War there developed in Trinidad and Tobago an awareness of the need to break away from the imperial economic pattern through the development of manufacturing. The movement toward economic reality was given expression in two ordinances passed on the same day, March 16, 1950: the income tax (in aid of industry) ordinance and the aid to pioneer industries ordinance.

These laws provided for extensive tax concessions to manufacturing plants, especially newly established ones. They provided for initial and depreciation allowances, freedom from customs duties on machinery, and raw materials for new establishments.

In a way this legislation is as significant in the economic history of Trinidad and Tobago as the Cedula of 1783. The cedula encouraged mining and agriculture, but there was a fundamental distinction in the legislation of 1950. As a condition of entry, Spain demanded loyalty. The more recent legislation could make no such demand. Whereas the former sought manpower, the latter sought capital. Yet even after the achievement of independence, vested interests continued to resist legislation capable of achieving that end. It was only after the 1967 failure of sterling as a reserve currency (for the second time since World War II) that opposition diminished to an appreciable extent.

With absorption into the British system, Trinidad and Tobago developed the standard colonial relationship with Britain as banker, financier, and trading partner. With the development of the sterling area after the monetary crisis of 1931, Trinidad and Tobago formally became a part of the area and was required to maintain its currency reserves and banking balances in London. The balances of the colonies at the outbreak of the Second World War amounted to about £500 million, the greater part of which was invested in the United Kingdom.

The monetary system of the first half of the twentieth century as it affected the colonies was such that sterling was the standard currency, and all colonial currencies were pegged to it. Reserves were held and invested in the United Kingdom. Monetary management therefore became simply an automatic consequence of the management of sterling. There were, of course, no restrictions on the movement of sterling within the sterling area. These were the essential features of the colonial financial and monetary system in 1950, when legislation attempted the first significant step in attracting capital for investment outside the traditional fields of colonial development.

The legislation allowed liberal tax concessions, wholly unrelated to performance in employment, effective resource use, or reinvestment of profits. One of its more extraordinary features was the incentive provided for speedy repatriation of profits, an effect in new industries of the provision requiring distributions to be within two years of the end of the "pioneer period" in order to qualify for exemption.

The intent of the legislation was to attract British investors and British capital in the same way the tariff structure favored importing British goods. The intention was to make it more profitable for the firm producing for Trinidad and Tobago markets to set up branch operations there. But, as Trinidad and Tobago had no tax-paring arrangement with the United Kingdom, branches remitting profits to the United Kingdom subjected the parent company to taxation there. What happened was that the Trinidad and Tobago treasury was losing revenues to the United Kingdom. The firm benefited only to the extent that it increased its capital holdings in Trinidad and Tobago by reinvesting or converting profits into capital in Trinidad and Tobago; the benefit to the United Kingdom shareholders was therefore only slight.

It should be pointed out that the same tax benefits were available to the Trinidad and Tobago investor; but his benefits were limited by lack of experience in the manufacturing field, lack of other than local markets, and dependence on technology that did not allow him to fully exploit his cost advantages in labor. Moreover, because the important decisions of financial institutions were always made by their head offices abroad, policies were based not on local opportunities and needs but on those of the home country.

Imperial Preferences

With integration into the sterling area, Trinidad and Tobago was also incorporated into the system of imperial preferences established by the Imperial Economic Conference in Ottawa in 1932. The system allowed free entry into Britain of commonwealth products and free entry of, or preferential duty rates for, British products. The system applied to all commonwealth countries in all trading with one another. This protectionist measure was in reaction to the period of free trade ascendancy in the United Kingdom that ended with the depression following the collapse of 1929.

The system of imperial preferences was a mutually beneficial arrangement but one that preserved the competitiveness of United Kingdom products, mainly manufactured goods, in commonwealth and empire markets. The advantage for commonwealth and empire products lay almost exclusively in primary commodities. Following these agreements were the commodity agreements in such areas as copper, rubber, lead, sugar, tea, and tin, which allowed colonies to maintain reasonably stable prices.

The aim of the system of preferences and commodity agreements was not, of course, to achieve structural transformation but rather to attain income stability within the context of ultratraditional trade relationships.

The Currency Board

In 1950 the currency board was instituted, and all the British colonial territories came within its jurisdiction. Although its principal and almost sole function was to issue notes and coins, the board became the standard instrument of monetary management throughout the colonial empire; it was the mechanism that brought all British colonies under a common sterling exchange standard. It has been argued in favor of the currency board that it provided the colonies with a completely convertible currency with a guaranteed parity and that it offered the security necessary for private investment. This was indeed so. In the context of the imperial system, however, the benefits were simply the equivalent of the benefits of access to British markets and the protection of the Royal Navy.

The currency board had two major weaknesses. First, currency circulation was determined by external factors, chiefly the volume of trade. Sterling had to be used to purchase the currency issued by the board, and in order to obtain sterling, there had to be sales in sterling markets. The second weakness was that the regulations governing its operation called for 100 percent note cover. This cover had to be in sterling securities that had to be purchased within the sterling area but outside the jurisdiction of the issuing board. The portfolios of the currency boards were all managed by the crown agents for the colonies in London. Within the theory of the imperial system this resulted in a sharing of savings within the area. In practice, however, the savings of the less developed areas tended to gravitate toward the more developed areas with their capital markets and available avenues for investment. The principle of cumulative causation applied unchecked.

Prior to the passing of the banking acts in 1964, Trinidad and Tobago's monetary arrangements had six main characteristics:
1. The currency was issued by a currency board, the key instrument (such as it was) of monetary control.
2. The board comprised representatives of nine governments, one independent and eight colonial.
3. The board's portfolio was managed not by the board but by crown agents for the colonies in London.
4. About 90 percent of the note cover had to be in sterling securities representing savings invested abroad.
5. The issue and redemption of the currency was automatic and bore no relation to prices, wages, credit, employment, or balance of payments.
6. A significant proportion of the money supply was not currency but bank credit over which the currency board had absolutely no control.

It was clearly necessary that more attention should focus on monetary management in the economic life of the country. What management there was before 1964 was fragmented and uncoordinated. Foreign exchange regulations were administered by the Ministry of Finance. The government accounts were kept in a commercial bank. The public debt was managed by the accountant general and the investment section of the Ministry of Finance. Reforms were still some time away, but the problems that made them necessary were at last beginning to be identified and marked for future action.

TOWARD FEDERATION
The period 1950-1956 was one of acute frustration. The widespread demand for democratic rule that the Moyne Commission recognized as early as 1937 had been only partially realized. World War II had slowed the movement toward self-government, but at the same time it intensified the demand for social and political reform. The Constitution of 1950 became, therefore, a symbol of successful pressuring in a flood

tide of political expectations.

The major political objective at this time was not independence but federation of the British West Indies as the first step toward wider Caribbean unity. The Caribbean already constituted a museum piece in the modern world with its insularity, fragmentation, and administrative duplication. The future members of the federation consisted of many islands, each having to maintain a complete system of government, internal and external.

When the urge to unite began to gain strength, it sprang from the twin desire for nationhood and economic development. Thus, following various other proposals, the Caribbean Congress of Labour proposed in 1938 a federation of the whole British Caribbean area including the Bahamas and the mainland areas of British Guiana and British Honduras. As it turned out, the federation did not include these three; still, it might have succeeded had it enjoyed vigorous and diligent assistance from the United Kingdom.

However, it was quite clear to the colonies themselves, as it was in the case of the union of Tobago with Trinidad, that the British government was not going to bear the heavy initial costs of setting up the necessary communications and administrative network to sustain the long-term economic development of the area. What was essential and what was continually ignored was the liquidation of the colonial economic system and the substitution of the economics of nationhood. And in this absolutely essential requirement for the regeneration of West Indian society, the British government was determined not to play a positive role.

The Rise of the PNM

In Trinidad and Tobago between 1950 and 1956, the movement toward self-government and social and economic reform became bogged down in political disorder, selfishness, and rising racism. Conspicuously absent was a political party of genuinely national representation with the capability of being infused with the discipline and organization necessary to carry out a comprehensive program of responsible reform.

If any further proof was necessary to demonstrate the need for such a party, it came with the postponement of the general elections due to have taken place in 1955. In response to the entire condition of lassitude, indirection, and mismanagement, the People's National Movement

(PNM) was launched in January 1956.

The major planks of the PNM platform were political education and morality in public office. The party cut across racial lines but drew its greatest support from people of African and mixed descent—urban organized labor, middle-income groups, clerks, teachers, civil servants, and agricultural workers (except sugar workers, most of whom are of East Indian descent). The PNM was hardly a reincarnation of Uriah Butler's movement, nor was party leader Eric Williams even a remote political disciple of Butler. In the early days of the PNM, however, *The Trinidad Guardian* (which at the time was hostile to the radical elements in the party) characterized Dr. Williams as "the lineal descendant of that bearded demogogue."

The main opposition to the PNM gathered around personalities: A. P. T. James in Tobago, Albert Gomes with most of his support in the essentially European-descended business community, and Victor Bryan in northeastern Trinidad.

Bhadase Saggan Maraj sought to unify people of East Indian extraction through a curious mixture of race, religion (Hindu Mahasabha), patronage, and terror. Maraj fell by the wayside, and was replaced by the current opposition, the Democratic Labor Party, led by the highly respected Dr. Rudranath Capildeo, a barrister and former lecturer in mathematics at the University of London.

Reflecting the great nationalist movements that were changing the face of the world and led by the region's most distinguished historian, Dr. Eric Williams, the PNM introduced new style and direction to the country's political life. The style was intellectual, the direction nationalistic. It attracted men of integrity and reputation, including Sir Learie Constantine, the first chairman of the party, and Dr. Patrick Solomon, the deputy political leader, a prominent figure in the earlier movement for constitutional reform.

In the general election of September 24, 1956, there developed a dramatic confrontation between the new and the old. The PNM represented the new world of the disciplined political party armed with a constitution and platform and presenting a clear-cut alternative to the electors. It was the new world of educating the electorate rather than playing upon its lack of sophistication. PNM demanded immediate self-government based on a bicameral legislature and a ministerial system of government. It called for a federation of the British West Indies with dominion status within five years of its establishment. The party promised honesty in the public service, local governmental reform, and a program of political education for the people, and it emphasized the need for physical and economic planning.

The result was smashing victory for the PNM. Of the twenty-four elective seats, PNM won thirteen. The constitution provided, however, that two additional members be named by the governor-general. The secretary of state for the colonies instructed him not to use this power to frustrate the will of the electorate. Accordingly, the governor, on the advice of Dr. Williams, who as head of the party became chief minister, appointed two members of the PNM to complete the legislative council. The stage was set for the final move forward. However, what should have been a smooth transfer of power turned out to be as rough a passage as the country had ever encountered in its political evolution.

New Tobago Policy

Even now there continues to exist much misunderstanding regarding the concept of the unitary state. The obvious error in the order-in-council that united Trinidad and Tobago in 1898 tended to vitiate the entire instrument setting out the constitutional relationship between the two islands. Clearly, such a result must have been symptomatic of a much deeper cause involving social, political, and psychological attitudes indigenous to the smaller island.

In its relationship with Trinidad and the United Kingdom, Tobago for a long time suffered from a kind of dual colonialism. The smaller island seemed a poor, barely tolerated dependency of the larger. Therefore, to most of the other islands, with the exception of Grenada, a postfederation unitary statehood that included Trinidad implied either subordination to Trinidad or the displacement of British with Trinidadian colonialism.

A. P. T. James, the first elected representative for Tobago under the system of adult franchise, repeatedly complained of Tobago's status, and until the People's National Movement gained power, this was the sentiment of the overwhelming majority of the island's inhabitants.

The PNM's first significant step toward rehabilitating Tobago is seen in a special section of the party's 1956 *Elections Manifesto.* Recognizing the special needs, problems, and potential of the island, the party specifically pledged to promote the following:

An efficient steamer service between Trinidad and Tobago.

Around-the-island road transport.

An expanded electricity service.

An expanded water distribution system.

Greater publicity for the recreational amenities and natural beauty of the island.

Direct communication between Tobago and the outside world by West Indian and international steamship lines.

Increased facilities for secondary education.

Marketing facilities for peasant farmers and fishing cooperatives.

Minor industries based upon agricultural products.

Provision for the ordinary amenities of civilization in all districts, such as postal services, district nurses, telephone communications, and library services.[11]

The PNM also pledged to set up a special Ministry of Tobago Affairs.[12]

The second step in the rehabilitation of Tobago occurred in 1957 when the chief minister, who was also minister of Tobago affairs, appointed a planning team to collaborate with the Colonial Development and Welfare Organization. A plan was prepared, and while efforts to persuade the United Kingdom government to assist in its financing proved fruitless, strenuous efforts were made toward implementing it.

The third step was the constitutional provision for minimum parliamentary representation, which counterbalanced Tobago's sparse population and comparative isolation from the administrative center of Trinidad.

More important than all these, however, was the change in attitude arising from the advent of a new philosophy of government, characterized most clearly by the PNM's pledge to develop the country's full agricultural potential and arrest urban migration.

The First Five-Year Plan

The economic climate just prior to federation was one of rising expectations. The movements in world petroleum prices were reflected in in-

11. PNM *Elections Manifesto*, 1956.
12. By 1969, however, there was once more growing discontent over the operation of the machinery of government. Talk of secession, common in the pre-PNM era, was revived.

creasing government revenues, and although there had been temporary setbacks, as in the pronounced decline in oil prices in 1948 and 1949, the trend was generally upward.

It was against this background that the first five-year-plan was introduced in 1958 by Chief Minister Eric Williams and the minister of planning and development. Adopting the language of the PNM *Elections Manifesto* of 1956, the chief minister described the principal features of the economic development of the country as follows:

The domination of the oil, sugar, and asphalt industries.

The underdevelopment of such areas as St. Andrew-St. David, Tobago, Nariva-Mayaro, Ortoire-Moruga.

The limited contribution of pioneer industries to employment and national output.

The existence of considerable underemployment, amounting to 14 out of every 100 persons employed.[13]

He noted the chief economic need as a large number of new jobs, development of the resources of the entire country, and expansion of existing industries and introduction of new ones.

The capital cost of the program over the five-year period was to be $191 million. The emphasis was to be on expansion of basic industries, particularly agriculture. The 1930s and the 1940s had been dark decades for the country's agriculture. Sugar and cocoa had been affected by declining world prices, cocoa had been further atrophied by disease, and the U.S. bases had induced labor away from the land. It was therefore imperative that agriculture expand at a faster rate if it was to afford the necessary contribution to employment.

The development program, 1958-1962, marked the first attempt at development planning in Trinidad and Tobago. A previous program had been prepared in 1955 by the government of 1950-1956 but had not been implemented, owing to that government's defeat by the PNM in the elections of 1956. The program recognized structural weaknesses in the economy and sought to change the emphasis in public expenditure. For example, the plan called for: increased assistance to the small agricultural producer through subsidies, marketing facilities, essential services, and improved water supplies; greater help for the cane farmer

13. Introduction to 1958 to 1962 Five-Year Development Program.

through mechanical aids to cultivation and control of the froghopper; and improvements in health facilities, education, and housing subsidies. Also, for the first time since the union of Trinidad and Tobago, the special position and problems of Tobago were fully recognized.

However, while there were distinct departures within the colonial economic and financial framework, there was no attempt to alter the framework itself, and adjustments in the relationships within the domestic and social scene did not extend to the country's external relationships. Dependence on the metropolitan country in financial, monetary, and commercial policies remained a fundamental assumption.

The federal issue was a many-sided one, involving relations of Trinidad and Tobago with the federal government, the United States and British governments, and the other West Indian governments participating in the federation. It can safely be said that no two states held the same position on the structure of the federation and the function of the federal government. The divergence of views is dramatized in a statement made on February 22, 1960, to the Jamaica House of Representatives by Mr. Norman Manley, premier of Jamaica:

On the one hand there is the view proposed by the Government of Trinidad and Tobago that the Federal Government should at once or shortly after achieving independence take full control over the economy of the entire Federal area, it being argued that only a powerful and centrally directed economic coordination and interdependence can meet the needs of the West Indies at the time. On the other hand there is the view propounded by the Government of Jamaica that the Federation should start with no more than the essential powers needed for it to gain recognition as a political entity acceptable to international agencies and more particularly to the British Commonwealth of Nations.[1]

In the Jamaican view, the constitution itself was to be flexible in scope. It provided machinery for amendment, making it possible for the federal center to expand as convenience and necessity dictated. It also allowed the federal government, with the consent of the units concerned, to take over the administration of special services in the interests of efficiency and economy.

Jamaica's answer to federal control of the economy was unequivocally negative. To quote further from Manley's statement:

Meanwhile there has developed and crystallized in Jamaica a strong body of opinion drawn from all political parties and all sections of society which is entirely opposed to Jamaica agreeing to continue in a Federation moving into independence in which by transferring to the Federal Centre all the factors of economic control there would be created a serious and far-reaching disruption of Jamaica's attempt at developing and modernizing her own economy. Jamaica, which has for 21 years led the way in movement towards West Indian independence, would not be a party to holding back the demand for West Indian independence at the present time. Either a way has to be found to reconcile these differences or a new basis without the existence of the present Federation

1. Jamaica House of Representatives, Statement by N. W. Manley, February 22, 1960, p. 1.

has to be found for achieving West Indian independence at the earliest possible date.[2]

It was an ominous statement, with all the undertones of a threat to withdraw from the federation. There were other aspects of the federal structure that the Jamaican premier considered in need of adjustment: representation; the exclusive and concurrent lists; delegation of functions by units to the federal government; common services and technical assistance; machinery for consultation between the federal government and units; the customs union; and finance and taxation. The list was long, but the basic principle was minimal power for the federal government to prevent the "serious and far-reaching disruption of Jamaica's attempt at modernizing her own economy."

Jamaica was convinced that she possessed a degree of sophistication in economic management that the other members of the federation did not even understand, let alone possess, and that the circumstances of the Jamaican economy were such that federal experimentation could do irreparable damage. The situation was aggravated by the tendency of the federation's prime minister, Sir Grantley Adams, to make statements in jest that served merely to exacerbate differences within the federation. Illustrating the point is the following extract from a news report of an address by the prime minister in New York under the auspices of the Caribbean League of America:

Mr. Moore's second question stated: "How can you as Prime Minister foster the development of Federal National consciousness when you make such insular and provincial comparisons as: 'The Barbadians are the most intelligent and industrious in the West Indies'; 'The average Trinidadian would rather sing a calypso than do any hard work'; 'A super-dynamic personality being a Barbadian' etc."

The Prime Minister's answer: "You would not think that he (pointing to Mr. Moore) is a Barbadian!"

Mr. Moore's rejoinder: "I am a Caribbean, now a Caribbean-American."

Prime Minister: "Now, really, do you know any Trinidadian who wouldn't rather sing a calypso than do any hard work?"

Mr. Moore: "Yes, I do. There is one right there—Mr. Clouden—and I know many others."

Prime Minister: "Would you deprive a man of the right to make a little joke?"[3]

The little jokes were obviously not going down well, and the situation grew progressively more serious.

2. *Ibid.*, p. 2.
3. West Indies News Service, Release (New York, October 26, 1959).

While Jamaica's major concern was over the federal government's actual or potential economic power, in Trinidad and Tobago there was anxiety over the federal government's attitudes toward the territory's political life. In government circles there was fear that the federal government, weak, exposed, and ineptly led, would become a pawn of foreign governments, particularly Britain and the United States.

THE FEDERAL STRUCTURE

The case for West Indian unity has been stated often enough to require only a brief recapitulation. Its bases are, unlike those of the colonial office, mainly economic rather than political or administrative and are clearly set forth in the *Economics of Nationhood:*

The case for economic integration of the West Indian territories rests less on the enlargement of the market which it will make possible than on the opportunity which it will provide for the more efficient use of the resources—human and material—of the Area as a whole in the interests of the Area as a whole.

It is true that there is no necessary correlation between the size of the national market and productivity per head of population. If there were, India, with a population of 400 million, would not have one of the lowest per capita incomes, while New Zealand, with a little over 2 million, has one of the highest in the world. Nevertheless, all the evidence seems to point to a minimum size of between 2 million and 3 million being necessary for the "take-off" into sustained economic growth.

Individually, the West Indian territories are a long way from such a minimum size; but, collectively, they provide the basis for a successful, if concerted, effort. It is clearly in their interests that, in the future, there should be a properly coordinated policy of economic development. This implies the introduction of the necessary instruments of economic integration and development appropriate to West Indian conditions—customs union, freedom of movement of labor and capital throughout the Federation, a single West Indian currency, a Central Bank, to name but a few.[4]

When the federation eventually came into being, one of the primary causes of its quick demise was the failure of the British government to discharge the responsibilities attached to the position it had maintained in the area for several centuries. In fact, it may be said that the United Kingdom, having assisted in the formation of a weak and ineffectual federation, played an equally prominent role in its foundering.

After many years of discussion, proposals, and counterproposals, the

4. *Economics of Nationhood* (Trinidad: Government Printery, 1959), p. 16.

Federation of the British West Indies was inaugurated on February 18, 1958. Table 4.1 lists the members of the federation and their respective areas and populations.

The instruments that brought about the federation were similar to those used in uniting Tobago and Trinidad in 1898. First, there was an enabling act, the Caribbean Federation Act of 1956, passed by the United Kingdom Parliament, empowering the queen to set up by an order-in-council the necessary federal institutions: a federal government, a federal legislature, and a federal supreme court.

Following the act of 1956 was the West Indies (Federation) Order-in-Council of 1957. The order-in-council provided for the establishment of a federal legislature consisting of a house of representatives and a senate, a federal executive, a federal supreme court, and a federal public service.

The portion of the order-in-council of greatest significance is a schedule consisting of two parts, the exclusive list and the concurrent list. The essence of a federal system is that separate jurisdictions arise from

Table 4.1. Members of the Federation of the West Indies

Territory	Area (square miles)	Population (mid-1956 estimate)	
Barbados	166		228,000
Jamaica and dependencies	4,677	Jamaica	1,564,000
		Dependencies	13,410 (1955)
Trinidad and Tobago	1,980		743,000
Leeward Islands:			
Antigua and Barbuda	171		53,000
St. Kitts-Nevis-Anguilla	153		54,800
Montserrat	32		14,400
Windward Islands:			
Dominica	305		63,800
Grenada	133		89,100
St. Lucia	238		89,000
St. Vincent	150		77,600

Source: Morley Ayearst, *The British West Indies* (London: Allen & Unwin, 1960), p. 12.

two distinct governments (federal and state), each embodying prescribed legislative and fiscal authority; provisions are made so that where powers overlap, one is to prevail over the other. However, these provisions are of little importance unless specifically related to the subject in the lists. In the case of the West Indian Federation, income tax on emoluments and allowances, for example, was included in the exclusive list of the federal government but was limited to federal officials and employees. Income tax also appeared on the concurrent list, but it was subject to the restriction that within five years of inception it could not be imposed on persons other than federal officers or employees.

Similarly, customs and excise duties appeared on the concurrent list but were subject to Articles 94 and 95 of the constitution, which together with Article 93 limited federal revenues to a maximum of $9,420,000, barely enough to sustain minimum common services such as defense, the regional shipping service, the University of the West Indies, and the basic federal institutions.

This constraint upon federal expenditures was to continue for a period of five years, when there was to be a constitutional review conference. By that time, of course, federation had come and gone.

FEDERAL WEAKNESSES

Timing

The movement toward self-government, especially in the larger territories of the area, gathered too much momentum for federation to overcome. Representative governments had come into being and had either achieved or were on the threshold of achieving responsible government. These governments were committed not only to improving the living standards of their citizens but also to the exhilarating experience of home rule itself. At the very moment when many of the territories were moving toward the end of the long and sometimes bitter struggle for self-assertion, a new rival for authority, the federal government, appeared on the scene. Even with the cohesiveness of hard times and small expectations, a new system is difficult to establish. The West Indian Federation was attempting to establish itself in a period of rapid change and great expectations. Since it appeared to slow the tempo of beneficial effects, the federation seemed to impede progress.

The British Role

Given the serious obstacles to federation often pointed out by Great Britain's own representatives (some of the obstacles the direct result of British policy such as the imperial pattern of trade and development), and given the compelling need for unity in the area, the British government ought to have taken more positive action to assist the federation.

Federal Leadership

Even without financial resources, there were two obvious issues on which the federal government—through effective leadership—could have generated popularity: Chaguaramas and independence itself. In both cases political maneuvering had displaced leadership.

Too often political differences were permitted to impair relationships completely. To this day, in fact, West Indian leaders have not found ways to communicate in time of crisis. The example of the emergency hot line between Moscow and Washington is an instructive one for the West Indies.

Admittedly, federal authority was extremely limited at the time. The fact is, though, that federal leaders failed to make use of the authority they did have. Given such a condition, the federation could make little impact. When Jamaica, with the concurrence and assistance of the United Kingdom, decided to withdraw from the federation, the federal government was considered so inconsequential that it was not even consulted.

THE CAPITAL SITE

The test case for the federation was to be the decision on the federal capital site, an issue that had taken shape even before federation. The choice of a capital site had always been a major point of contention in forming the federation. Several conferences had recommended various sites, including Barbados, Grenada, and St. Lucia. The difficulties in selection led to the appointment of a capital site commission on June 1, 1956. The commission, whose chairman was Sir Stephen Luke, was given the following framework:

To submit recommendations to the Standing Federation Committee on the three most suitable sites in order of preference for the capital, bearing in mind the following factors:
(1) political and social sentiment throughout the area;
(2) the convenience of the site in relation to the Federal area;

(3) the availability of land both for immediate buildings and for future expansion;

(4) the cost of the necessary buildings on the selected site and other works;

(5) the suitability of communications by sea, air, cable, telephones and road;

(6) the services available

(a) general accommodation

(b) hotels

(c) general urban facilities

(d) water supplies

(e) electricity and power

(f) educational facilities

(g) the availability of suitable recruits for subordinate posts in the Federal Service.[5]

There was confusion from the outset. The commission reported:

We found that there was some doubt as to what exactly we were intended to do. One view was that it would be possible for us, within our terms of reference, to recommend three sites, all on the same island; another that it was our business to recommend the three islands that we considered the most suitable for the capital. We adopted a middle course.[6]

This middle course led to recommending the three most suitable islands in order of preference: Barbados, Jamaica, and Trinidad. Trinidad, otherwise the most suitable, was given a low rating on the grounds of "the instability of that island's politics and the low standard accepted in its public life." "To put the capital near Port-of-Spain," the Commission reported, "would, in our opinion, be to run a very great risk, which need not be run."[7] The capital would be corrupted by the unhealthy state of Trinidad's politics.

Before the next scheduled federal conference, the PNM came to power. The conference that was convened for choosing the site demonstrated its approval of the new government of Trinidad and Tobago by selecting Trinidad for the capital site. The location chosen was the Northwest Peninsular, including the area occupied by the United States naval base at Chaguaramas. This was done in complete disregard of the wishes of the PNM, which in its 1956 manifesto had pledged respect for international agreements and had specifically referred to the 1941

5. *Report of the British Caribbean Federal Commission*, Colonial no. 328 (London: HMSO, 1956), p. 3.

6. *Ibid.*, p. 3.

7. *Ibid.*, p. 22.

United States Leased Bases Agreement. Nevertheless, the conference insisted that the Northwest Peninsular was "the only suitable site" in Trinidad.

In Trinidad and Tobago, however, there was suspicion that the Chaguaramas site had been chosen for the very reason that it could not be obtained, a move that would open the door for selection of another island. Some attributed the affair to the wily Sir Grantley Adams, whose preference for Barbados was public knowledge. Others felt that it was a masterful political gambit by Premier Manley of Jamaica to highlight the presence of bases occupied by a foreign power and to give impetus to the movement toward nationhood.

The situation was made increasingly serious by the clumsy handling of the issue by the British and United States authorities. They appeared to be treating the West Indian leaders patronizingly, even contemptuously. It was this attitude that led the chief minister of Trinidad and Tobago, Dr. Williams—ever unhappy over his political position since the choice—to devote his attention to solving the quandary.[8]

After some study of the files, Dr. Williams became aware of the stand that had been made by the British colonial governor, Sir Hubert Young. Young had rigorously opposed the location of bases, the length of the lease, and the extent of the powers conceded to the U.S. Government. As a democratic nationalist leader, he considered it morally and politically indefensible to maintain a position less concerned about the country's best interests than the one adopted long before by an autocratic British colonial governor. Freed from moral reservations, Dr. Williams was able to join his federal colleagues, who were as surprised at the vigor of his attack as the British and the Americans. He later obtained the approval of both government and party for the reversal of policy and pursued the struggle unrelentingly when those who had raised the issue appeared to have lost their stomach for the campaign.

The first reaction of the British government, through which the West Indian leaders were constitutionally bound to raise the issue, was negative. The British government was nevertheless prevailed upon to con-

8. At the third meeting of the Standing Federation Committee held in 1957 from May 6 to 17, Dr. Williams said, "If Trinidad and Tobago supports the resolution, she will be exposed to the charge of using the S.F.C. to break international commitments. If Trinidad opposed it, she would be suspected of trying to thrust some other site on her Federal partners."

vene a meeting with representatives of the United States government. The meeting took place on July 16, 1957. Though it was clear that the Americans had come with inflexible positions, it was equally clear that the dramatic change of policy by the Trinidad and Tobago delegation had its effect. The delegation from the West Indies was no longer pleading for the generosity of large nations; it was assailing the moral foundations of an agreement forced upon a small captive people.

An arrangement was made to appoint a joint commission of experts, which was instructed to "investigate all angles of the B.W.I. request to make Chaguaramas available, taking into full account military and economic considerations."[9]

Briefly, the committee's report, issued after federation had taken place, found Chaguaramas the most suitable site for a naval base, a fact that failed to dispel the conviction that Chaguaramas was also the most suitable site for the capital. The report cited the historical role that the base had played during the course of World War II but made no real effort to assess its future. The committee also found that there were five other suitable sites for a base, the best being Irois Bay, which would cost an estimated $132 million if brought to the operational level of Chaguaramas.

Both the British and American authorities thereupon issued statements to the effect that they considered this the end of the matter. Within two weeks of the report's release, the British government unilaterally stated its decision not to ask the United States to move the base and to make no contribution whatever to any such operation. The British took the stand that the report had indicated that there was no alternative to Chaguaramas.[10] Opposition parties at both the federal level and unit levels then proceeded to agitate the issue in the hope of gaining political capital out of the apparent failure of the West Indian leaders to make any headway on the capital site. While the federal government wavered, however, the nationalist movement in Trinidad and Tobago enthusiastically took up the issue. Addressing a public meeting on July 17, 1959, on the subject "From Slavery to Chaguaramas," Dr. Wil-

9. *Report of the Chaguaramas Joint Commission* (London: HMSO, 1958), p. 2.
10. In reply to the British stand, the *PNM Weekly,* organ of the ruling party, insisted there were five alternative sites to Chaguaramas and accused the British government of fraud.

liams said, "You make it clear, all you West Indians, that if you had to choose between Chaguaramas as an American base and Chaguaramas as a West Indian capital, the West Indian capital comes first and it is the American base that has to move.[11]

In perhaps the best political speech of his entire career, Williams faced squarely the issue of self-government raised by the Chaguaramas affair. Meanwhile, for fear of losing its parliamentary support, the federal government had begun to soft-pedal the issue and, without consulting the leaders of the unit governments, made an accommodation with the British and United States governments.[12]

The essence of the accommodation that was announced in the federal House of Representatives was that the matter of the capital site would be deferred for ten years, the United Kingdom and United States governments having given assurances that they would then be prepared to review the situation in the light of "any changes in methods of warfare which might make it unnecessary to retain Chaguaramas as a naval base." The announcement, made by the federal prime minister, Sir Grantley Adams, on June 16, 1958, preserved the majority for the federal government but did not resolve the issue. Moreover, it exposed the weakness of the federal government not only in its relations with the parliamentary opposition but, worst of all, also in its relations with the British and United States governments. The problem was in no way alleviated when the British government, which had retained responsibility for the foreign relations of the federation, not long afterward gave what it termed an "entrustment" of the conduct of foreign affairs to the federal government. Thus, for the conduct of foreign relations, the federal government was made a delegate of the British government.

The accommodation served to strengthen the determination of the Trinidad and Tobago government, which was now interested not only in the release of the capital site but also in a comprehensive review of the entire agreement. Leaders in Trinidad and Tobago recognized the

11. Dr. Eric Williams, "From Slavery to Chaguaramas" (Trinidad: PNM Publishing, 1959), p. 15.
12. The Federal Labour Party, which controlled the government, had only twenty-two of forty-five seats in Parliament. The three independents who held the balance of power had declared themselves in general support of the government on the Chaguaramas issue, but the federal government was nonetheless unsure of their loyalty.

political value of the issue and the strength of their position against the background of the pattern of base agreements that were beginning to appear in other parts of the world. Perhaps the most unfortunate aspect of the issue was that it strengthened support for the Trinidad and Tobago government at the expense of the federal government. It allowed a legitimately federal issue to become a local one, at a time when federalism could ill afford to squander political capital. Through its timorous conduct on the issue, the federal government missed an excellent opportunity to weld together the variegated loyalties in the federation. It was left to the Trinidad and Tobago government to carry the main burden of the struggle for national recognition. The final negotiations for the release of the area took place between the Trinidad and Tobago and United States governments, with the federal government being present as a mere observer.

COLLAPSE OF FEDERATION

The weakness of the federation at the constitutional level was matched by its political weakness. Jamaica, which from the beginning had found the federation useless for its own goals, was talking openly of secession; there was little federal effort to prevent such a move.

The federal constitution made no provision whatever for secession. Nonetheless, Britain in no way tried to dissuade leaders in Jamaica from holding a referendum on it. The vote favoring Jamaican secession manifested the extraordinary spectacle of one of the federation's eleven governments casually proposing to abrogate the constitution, to which the British Parliament agreed without so much as cocking an ear toward the other states.

After formalizing discussions with Jamaica, Britain agreed to its separation from the federation, whereupon the Trinidad and Tobago government adopted the stand that this was tantamount to dissolution of the federation. In the penetrating if unmathematical phrase of Eric Williams, "One from ten leaves zero." Trinidad and Tobago decided to proceed to independence alone but left the door open for reassociation with such islands as might wish it.

THE PREINDEPENDENCE ECONOMY

A major barrier to Trinidad and Tobago's economic well-being within the federation was the matter of the carried-over import-export policies, which the federation did not attempt to reform. Arrangements prior to independence are most strikingly illustrated by the fact that during the period 1956-1961 the total receipts from nonpetroleum exports went to finance the import of bare necessities, most of which came from outside the federation and much of which could have been produced in Trinidad and Tobago in the first place. No steps were taken to correct this during the federal period. In a sense this inactivity was Trinidad and Tobago's sacrifice to the West Indian Federation. The political goal at the time was, quite rightly, independence within the federation. Adjustments in the country's external relationships were therefore subordinate to the aims of the federation. Once subordinated, their importance diminished in both government policy and public consciousness. Hence, there was no economic or financial planning for independence. Geared to the expectation of independence within the federation, the people of Trinidad and Tobago, although anxious to undertake the responsibilities of independence, were psychologically unprepared for it.

Earnings of $99 million in 1961 from nonpetroleum exports went to purchase the imports shown in Table 4.2. Without oil, Trinidad and Tobago would have been unable to import motor vehicles, bicycles, books, machinery, alcoholic beverages, and tobacco, to mention only a few items, and would also have had to import oil products.

The predominance of the petroleum industry was reflected not only

Table 4.2. Selected Imports, 1961

Product	Millions of Dollars
Meat	13.9
Dairy products	14.5
Fish	3.2
Flour	10.9
Rice	7.0
Coffee, tea, cocoa	2.7
Fruit and vegetables	8.6
Medicines	4.7
Textiles	21.1
Footwear	6.7
Clothing	5.7

Source: Budget Speech in *Hansard Reports*, 1 (1961-1962): 668-669.

in the high proportion of the total value of exports (more than 80 percent) but also in the rate of increase in the value of petroleum exports and imports above all other commodities. Between 1956 and 1961 the total value of imports rose from $302 million to $575 million or by 92 percent. During the same period, imports of crude petroleum for refining increased from $87 million to $263 million or by more than 200 percent. Other imports rose by 45 percent. During the same period oil exports rose by 116 percent, while nonpetroleum exports other than oil increased by only 30 percent. Nonpetroleum imports were rising at a dangerously faster rate than nonpetroleum exports.

The policy of keeping import prices low facilitated the importation of food and manufactured goods, from Great Britain in particular, and developed in Trinidad and Tobago a propensity to import. Any increase in income was absorbed by a proportionally greater increase in imports, making the economy highly vulnerable to adverse movements in import prices or export receipts. This situation was illustrated by the severe depression that accompanied the collapse of cocoa and sugar, the country's two major crops, between the two world wars and by the acute domestic price increases that accompanied the disruption of trade during the Second World War.

The import policy is clearly reflected in the low rate of import duties, which averaged 11.8 percent of the total value of nonpetroleum imports over the period 1950-1959. The average rate for the other nine territories comprising the West Indies Federation was 13.3 percent, still rather low by international standards. The overall picture was one of basic structural weakness under existing fiscal arrangements.

In addition to encouraging consumption of imports, low tariffs brought the metropolitan view of overseas economic activity into full play, with imperial preferences fitting neatly into the pattern.

It was in the climate of economic disorder and bitterness deriving from the breakup of the West Indian Federation that the government of Trinidad and Tobago undertook the task of leading the country to independence. The task was further complicated by the opposition, who did not want Trinidad and Tobago to go it alone.

At a conference of organizations the draft constitution for the country was debated for three days. Issues that gave rise to the greatest controversy were fundamental rights, citizenship, the powers of the prime minister, and the appointment and dismissal of members of the judiciary. In response to opinions from the floor, the government agreed to the following modifications:

1. The insertion of a preamble, with a suitable reference to "Almighty God."

2. A careful examination of Section 2(1) with a view to extending the period of application for citizenship.

3. The insertion of a bill of rights similar to the Canadian bill of rights, with appropriate safeguards.

4. The disqualification of the chief justice as a possible acting governor-general.

5. An alteration in the composition of the Senate, without departing from the principle of representation of religious, social, and economic interests.

6. The tightening of the amendment procedure by requiring a satisfactory majority of both houses of Parliament.

7. Permitting appeals from decisions regarding the institution of election petition proceedings.

8. Amending the draft constitution to prevent Parliament from sitting more than five years except in the very limited circumstances to be specified.

Following this discussion, government representatives participated in a Joint Select Committee of Parliament, whose report was adopted by the House of Representatives on May 11, 1962. A delegation of government and opposition members then proceeded to London for final discussions with the British government.

There still existed sharp differences between the government and opposition wings of the Trinidad and Tobago delegation. Dispute centered on citizenship, fundamental rights, emergency powers, parliamentary appointments and other powers of the governor-general, delineation of constituencies, executive powers, the judiciary, appeals, the Judicial and Legal Service Commission, the public service, and the conduct of elections. It was a formidable enough area of disagreement to threaten the collapse of discussions in London, but statesmanship on the part of both government and opposition leaders surmounted internal differences. It was a fitting culmination to the struggle for independence, terminating with the application of the Independence Act and the Independence Constitution on August 31, 1962. (See Appendix 3.)

On August 31, 1962, Trinidad and Tobago came into possession of a flag, an anthem, and a coat of arms—status symbols of independence. As the new national flag came into view and a band struck up the new national anthem the entire crowd hesitated a moment, and then—as if rehearsed to respond on cue—broke into an incredible, jubilant roar. For at least that stirring moment, there was no doubt that the people of the islands had achieved a sense of national solidarity and destiny.[1]

Reminiscent of the inception of the short-lived West Indian Federation, independence began in a climate of rising expectations. Independence itself fosters expectations, and without reasonably rapid advancements in social and economic relations, there would have been little justification for breaking away from the relative security of the imperial system. Pressures for immediate benefits are even more intense in democratic countries with periodic elections.

However, while leaders of newly independent countries are anxious to comply with demands for immediate change, they must face up to the harsh realities of long-term planning. Constraints are manifold. In a society recently subordinated to metropolitan interests, knowledge (particularly scientific knowledge and technology) and techniques of organization, management, and human relations are at a premium. Labor is often indifferent, management incompetent, education unduly restrictive, and the social and intellectual climate stuffy and insular. The situation is compounded when the mass media are controlled either by foreigners or by a self-interested political elite.

Against this background, meaningful change, particularly economic change, is a hazardous activity. But such change is a necessity; the economics of colonialism must be transformed into the economics of independence.

The first requirement is the development plan, an example of which has already been described. It is the savings and investment program of the nation, and especially in newly independent countries the development plan must have social as well as economic implications. It must bring into the emerging dynamics of social and economic activity the portion of the population whose interests the colonial system tended systematically to neglect—in other words, the overwhelming majority.

1. Ivor Oxaal, *Black Intellectuals Come to Power* (Cambridge, Mass.: Schenkman, 1968), p. 1.

Independence and Economic Reform 2

Given such a precondition, the pursuit of development along classic laissez-faire lines becomes ridiculous.

It is of the utmost importance to recognize that in colonial systems it is political power that creates and defends privilege. If privilege is to give way to equality, political power must be used to promote and defend equality—not the equality superficially described as "spreading the wealth," but a more fundamental and humane equality, the basic characteristic of which is economic and social mobility.

The Spanish and the British colonists in Trinidad and Tobago admirably demonstrated the technique for creating an elite. The planter class was given land, the means of communication, cheap labor, and generous tax incentives. Similar incentives were later extended to emerging manufacturing interests under aid-to-pioneer-industries legislation. In both cases, the development that resulted was the kind that was hostile to social mobility in an economic and social milieu that was already nearly frozen solid.

Apart from the patently inadequate provisions for technical and higher education that date from colonial times, the Caribbean as a whole has, since independence, shown little will to come to grips with the fundamental problem of social and economic mobility. And recognition of the need is conspicuously lacking so far in development planning in Trinidad and Tobago.

The second, and equally important, requirement for the economics of independence is the redesign of the external and internal financial structure. Just as the metropolitan center maintained monetary control through the various elements of its financial system—for example, branch banks, the currency board, and the sterling exchange standard—the key to dissolution of monetary control is the central bank. Metropolitan interests transplanted into colonial areas are well aware of this fact and usually seek either to resist the establishment of a central bank or at least to keep it from attaining anything beyond minimum effectiveness.

Together with monetary changes the economics of independence also demands changes in the regulation of the international flow of capital. These may involve the treatment of public or private loan capital, private investment capital, remission of profits and interest, royalties, management charges, and various fees, as well as arrangements to preclude double taxation.

A third essential to the economics of independence is that of adjusting the structure of trade and tariffs. Briefly, this process involves the diversification of trade relationships outside the imperial pattern and the removal of the bias that previously subordinated the colonial economy to a role of captive supplier of raw materials and captive market for manufactured goods.

The fourth essential to the economics of independence is the transformation of the internal economic structure by transferring control of institutions from external to internal management, broadening the base of economic power, and opening up the entire structure to general participation by the population.

TARIFF REFORM

In 1962, for the first time in its history, the budget of Trinidad and Tobago served as an instrument of economic policy. Attention was focused principally on tariff reform. Apart from revenue considerations, the immediate objectives were to minimize imports of nonessential commodities, with the aim of freeing more foreign exchange for the purchase of capital goods; to provide a measure of protection to domestic manufacturers; to hold down food prices, especially on foods for which there were no local substitutes; and to minimize production costs.

The broader objectives were to achieve a more favorable balance in the external accounts, to stimulate agricultural and industrial diversification and production, and to lay the foundation for wider economic cooperation in the Caribbean.

The resulting tariff was a typical rate of 15 percent preferential, 25 percent general. The protective rate tended to be about 20 percent preferential, 30 percent general. The minimum rate was 5 percent preferential, 15 percent general.[1] Wherever possible, specific rates were changed to reflect invoiced value; where specific rates were retained, they were altered to agree with the new decimalized currency.

The rates on whiskey were increased by the equivalent of $3.50 per liquid gallon. The increase on rum was between $2.39 and $2.71 per gallon. There were corresponding increases on other alcoholic beverages as well as on tobacco and tobacco products.

The previous patchwork method of levying duty on motorcars was replaced by assessment on the basis of invoiced value. To encourage a local assembly industry, motor vehicles other than cars attracted a 10 percent lower duty if they were imported at least partly knocked down.

Other principal items altered from specific to invoiced value were firearms, poultry, coffee and coffee products, confections, and cocoa.

Coloring materials and paint products were amalgamated under single rates. Some of the items affected included footwear, prefabricated buildings, watches, clocks, phonographs and records, pianos and piano parts, domestic electrical appliances and parts, appliances for ships and motorcars, beverage and water coolers and parts, firearms, and cosmetics.

1. See also Combined Trade Classification List, 1965.

Other items were declared free of duty from all sources. They included the following: industrial apparatus and machinery for factory use;[2] agricultural tools and implements; field crates, picking bags, and juice preservatives for use in the citrus industry; containers for the packaging of local products; goods made from Sea Island Cotton bearing the mark of the West Indies Sea Island Cotton Association;[3] fishing nets and gear, fishing lines, wire fishhooks, seine, twine, synthetic netting, and pine tar for use in the local fishing industry; art supplies; string, wind, percussion, and other musical instruments not otherwise specified; insecticides and fungicides; soil conditioners; plumbing equipment; and printing supplies except those imported for resale.

The nature of protection afforded the local manufacturer can be inferred from the samples listed in Table 5.1. The guiding principle was to provide an adequate differential in favor of the local product without providing a shield for high cost and inefficient industries. The treatment of items regarded as basic foodstuffs as illustrated in the selection of items in Table 5.2. The Ministry of Agriculture, Industry, and Commerce was designated to keep under general review the standards, prices, and availability of all goods under tariff protection.[4]

Although the measures adopted in 1962 were hardly drastic, they were wide enough in scope and clear enough in orientation to represent a meaningful departure from colonialism, adopting a path of genuine reform of the country's economy. Incorporation of the surtax and the rounding-off of figures to conform to decimal currency facilitated the administrative processes involved with clearing goods from customs. The system was deliberately weighted against the importation of nonessential commodities to favor the development of local agriculture and industry and promote a favorable balance of payments.

TAX REFORM

The Purchase Tax
The tariff reforms of 1962 paved the way for the purchase tax of 1963,

2. A small tariff of 1 percent was reimposed in 1968 on the recommendation of a tripartite fiscal review committee.
3. This was done to encourage a dying West Indian industry using especially high-grade cotton.
4. By 1968 there was growing demand for a bureau of standards.

Table 5.1. Protective Tariff Increases, 1962

Manufactured Goods	Previous Rates		New Rates	
	Preferential	General	Preferential	General
Cotton grays	7.5%	15%	20%	30%
Cotton fabrics (white) bleaches, valued at 28¢ per sq. yd.	7.5% both + 12¢ per sq. yd.	15%	20% both + 5¢ per sq. yd.	30%
Cotton fabrics printed, valued at 36¢ per sq. yd.	7.5% both + 12¢ per sq. yd.	15%	20% both + 5¢ per sq. yd.	30%
Underwear and nightwear of knitted fabrics	11.5%	23%	15% + $2 per doz. garments	30%
Shirts knitted or made of knitted fabrics	11.5%	23%	15% + a protective surcharge	30%
Outerwear, knitted or made of knitted fabrics	11.5%	23%	20%	30%
Underwear and nightwear other than knitted	11.5%	23%	25%	35%
Shirts, nonknitted	11.5% + $5.75 per doz.	23%	20% + $5.00 per doz.	30%
	20.7% + $6.90 per doz.	32.2%	20% + $7.00 per doz.	30%
Outerwear, other than knitted	11.5%	23%	25%	35%
Wood, furniture and fixtures	11.5%	23%	25%	30%
Metal, furniture and fixtures	11.5%	23%	20%	30%
Furniture, n.e.s.*	11.5%	23%	20%	30%
Beer and ale	$1.05 per gal.	$1.68	$1.50 per gal.	$2.25
Rum, bottled, not overproof	$9.57 per gal.	$10.85	$11.96 per gal.	$13.56
Rum, bottled, other	$10.86 per gal.	$12.20	$13.58 per gal.	$15.25
Gin, bottled, not overproof	$17.25 per gal.	$18.15	$21.56 per gal.	$22.69
Gin, bottled, other	$20.25 per gal.	$21.15	$25.31 per gal.	$26.44
Poultry, killed or dressed	Free	$0.50	5%	10%
Coffee, roasted extracts	$0.04 per lb.	$0.12	15%	25%
Cocoa, powder	$0.04 per lb.	$0.12	15%	25%

Source: *Hansard Reports*, 1 (1961-1962):675-676.
*Not elsewhere specified.

Table 5.2. Basic Foodstuff Tariffs, 1962

	Previous Rates		New Rates	
Item	Preferential	General	Preferential	General
Cornmeal	$0.24	$0.48	$0.25	$0.50
Flour	Free per 196 lb.	$0.48	Free per 200 lb.	$0.50
Salt fish	Free per 100 lb.	$0.48	Free per 100 lb.	$0.50
Pickled pork	$0.25 per 100 lb.	$1.00	Same per 100 lb.	
Pickled meats—beef	$0.25 per 100 lb.	$1.00	Same per 100 lb.	
Butter	$0.0115 per lb.	$0.046	$0.015 per lb.	$0.045
Potatoes	$0.15 per 100 lb.	$0.90	$0.25 per 100 lb.	$0.75
Onions	$0.15 per 100 lb.	$0.90	$0.25 per 100 lb.	$0.75
Garlic	$0.003 per lb.	$0.006	$0.0025 per lb.	$0.007

Source: *Hansard Reports,* 1 (1961-1962):676.

which further restrained nonessential consumption. The purchase tax was not new to Trinidad and Tobago. Shortly after World War II the governor was empowered to impose such a tax on a number of specified commodities. The measure was inspired, no doubt, by the introduction of a similar measure in the United Kingdom. However, the tax was never put into effect in Trinidad and Tobago, and the reason is easy to imagine. A purchase tax in Trinidad and Tobago would have had the effect of a nonpreferential import duty running contrary to the system of commonwealth preferences.

In 1957 a 10 percent motor vehicles tax was imposed on certain classes of vehicles. It was in principle a purchase tax, except that it was payable upon registration rather than on purchase of the vehicle. In 1962 the rate was increased to a maximum 40 percent on any vehicles with market values exceeding $5,000, a minimum of 10 percent on vehicles valued below $3,000, and an intermediate rate of 30 percent. The tax also extended to certain consumer durables, alcoholic beverages, and luxury items, examples of which are shown in Table 5.3. Other items affected included locally manufactured and imported cigarettes.

Table 5.3. Purchase Tax, 1963

Items Taxed	Percent
Television sets	25
Radiophonographs, electrothermic apparatus, portable electric appliances	15
Phonographs and electric refrigerators	15
Other consumer durables: hot plates, toasters, excluding electric irons	10
Radio receivers for household use; nonelectric refrigerators and nonelectric record players	10
Perfumes and toilet waters above $1.00 per dozen; jewelry, cutlery of precious metal, cameras, watches and clocks of precious metals	10
Other watches and clocks	10

Source: *Hansard Reports*, vol. 1, part 1 (1962-1963), p. 919.

These additional measures became necessary not only for raising revenue but for the wider purpose of diverting resources from consumption to investment and production. As the minister of finance[5] pointed out in his budget speech, the real national income in 1960 was 41 percent greater than in 1956 and almost 100 percent greater than in 1951. In spite of a population increase of about 3 percent per year, real per capita income rose by about 58 percent between 1951 and 1961, a 35 percent increase occurring between 1956 and 1961.

In 1956, 87.2 percent of the total national income had gone to individuals (after direct taxation), and by 1960 this total had risen to 88.4 percent. As national income increased, the proportion of it accruing to individuals also increased. At the same time, the proportion of national income retained by local companies for investment decreased from 1.7 percent in 1956 to 0.7 percent in 1960. Government revenues, exclusive of indirect taxation, had also decreased. Clearly, the increase in national income was at the expense of government income and corporate investment. It was further adduced that this increase had been spent on private motoring, consumer durables, and international travel, which taken together represented an import content of nearly 100 percent.

The sort of criticism that the purchase tax measures encountered can

5. The author, who served in that post from 1961 to 1966. (Ed.)

be seen in the reply of the minister of finance in the budget debate of 1963:

Is it better to put a person to sell cars than to put him to build schools? Some people are saying that to create unemployment in the private sector is always worse than to create unemployment in the public sector. What about the motor repair establishments? If people tend to keep their cars longer because of the budget proposals and because of the purchase tax, is it not likely that they will require more attention to these cars in terms of maintenance services, and will there not be room for expansion of these services?

The 25 percent tax on television sets came in for severe criticism. To this the reply was given:

Representations have been made that the tax is likely to affect the introduction of this new service, which has been described as educational.[6] We do not accept that this is such an essential service that we can spend a large proportion of our resources on it. . . .

I think that the most fundamental criticism was sought to be made by the Honorable Member for Pointe-à-Pierre when he said that no principles were observed in the fixing of a lot of these taxes. Particularly he mentioned licenses, and in referring to the matter of purchase taxes he said that the Minister appeared to be paranoic, taxing things because he did not like them and, apparently, absolving things because he liked them. He went on to say that motor-cars were no longer luxuries, that he did not see how electrical appliances could be taxed, and that all of these things had become necessities. . . .

In support of the criticism which he made on what he considered to be the position adopted by the Government, he quoted from Professor Arthur Lewis. . . .

So now, if Honorable Members would permit me, I would go on to read the following paragraph and also additional quotations from the same Chapter which was referred to by the Honorable Member for Pointe-à-Pierre.

Professor Arthur Lewis went on:

"This analysis brings out as well the importance of political considerations in taxation. Most Governments find it easier to tax those who oppose them and to exempt those on whose support they rely. And this fact plays as large a part in determining the distribution of the tax burden as considerations of equity, of incentives or of savings. Yet the fact remains that in most of these economies it is impossible for the Government to play the role it needs to play in economic development unless it taxes all classes more heavily than they are taxed at present. The major political problem in most of these countries is to persuade the

6. A television network was set up in 1962 with a controlling interest held by Lord Thompson, who had previously purchased the *Trinidad Guardian*, the territory's leading daily newspaper, the *Sunday Guardian*, and the *Evening News*.

people that this is so, and to gain their consent to the necessary measures. The authoritarian governments are in this respect at an advantage in comparison with the democratic governments. ... The democratic governments are in greater difficulty. Here and there a great democratic leader is able to carry his people through a phase of relative privation for the sake of building up the nation and holds their confidence and enthusiasm. But such leaders are rare."[7]

I can quite understand why the Honorable Member for Pointe-à-Pierre omitted that paragraph. Professor Lewis goes on:

"In levying indirect taxes the principle is to put high rates upon luxury articles and other articles for which the demand is increasing rapidly, whether they are strictly luxury articles or not. The latter category is quite wide in some countries because the spread of westernisation is increasing rapidly the demand for such things as electrical appliances, radios, bicycles, motor transport, beer, cigarettes, gramophones or furniture. An import duty or excise tax of 100 percent of the wholesale value may be only 30 to 40 percent of the retail value. Some Governments are reluctant to levy 100 percent duties but quite a few duties at this level may be needed if the marginal rate of taxation is to be brought up to forty to fifty percent."[8]

That clearly demonstrates the reason why we heard nothing more from Professor Arthur Lewis than the particular paragraph we had.[9]

The estimated yield from the indirect taxation measures of 1963 was $11.5 million; together with measures to increase direct taxation by $5 million, they sought to increase revenues to just under 19 percent of gross domestic product (GDP).

The Income Tax Amendment

The principal objectives of the 1963 income tax legislation were: (1) safeguards against any appearance of retroactivity, (2) minimizing of evasion, (3) provision of an even flow of revenue throughout the year, and (4) the strengthening of tax administration.

The first enactment providing for taxation on incomes in Trinidad and Tobago was War Contribution Tax Ordinance No. 1 of 1917. The legislation was to expire at the end of one year but was extended by another enactment, this one known as War Tax on Incomes Ordinance No. 12 of 1918. The tax of 1918 expired at the end of that year but was immediately reincarnated in the form of the Tax on Incomes Ordinances of 1919, 1920, and 1921. In 1922 the income tax, like most

7. See W. Arthur Lewis, *The Theory of Economic Growth* (London: Allen & Unwin, 1955), p. 401.
8. *Ibid.*, p. 403.
9. *Hansard Reports*, vol. 1, part 1 (1962-1963), pp. 1312-1365.

temporary taxes, became a permanent feature by enactment of Income Tax Ordinance No. 8 of 1922. It remained virtually untouched until the introduction of the pay-as-you-earn system in 1958.[10] The law was a product of the commissioners of inland revenue in the United Kingdom and was intended to be a model for all of Britain's colonial territories. It was a simplified version of the British legislation and, like similar legislation in most other underdeveloped countries at the time, was most notable for its high exemption limits, generous allowances, and broad, well-marked avenues of evasion.[11]

The pay-as-you-earn system was designed to increase the efficiency of revenue collection, but it made no attempt to alter the structure of the legislation. Even at the time of the introduction of the original law in 1922 deficiencies were recognized, and the question of reform was debated from time to time. In 1963 the principle of reform was not itself in issue. As the minister of finance said in moving the amendment:

I think we can safely say that today nobody opposes reform—at least openly. The controversy which exists is in respect of the scope and timing of the reform. Some recognize that there is urgent need for these reforms, but consider that amendments should be reduced to the barest minimum which is compatible with increased revenue yields and a more efficient tax administration. Others think that reform should be postponed indefinitely until, as some have said, the economic climate of the country has become more propitious. But the point is [that] nobody opposes tax reform in respect of income tax legislation. . . . If one is to maintain some sort of equity and some sort of balance in the burdens which fall upon the community as a whole, then it is necessary at the time that you are looking at indirect tax proposals also to look at direct taxation.[12]

The need for the review of the income tax structure had in fact been recognized at the cabinet level prior to 1962, when expert services had been obtained from the United Kingdom. Early in 1962 the cabinet appointed a committee of officials to review and complete the work but failed to do so partly because of the lack of trained personnel at the time in the department of inland revenue.

10. This system was bitterly fought in Trinidad and Tobago by the opposition in Parliament, business interests, and the press. See *Hansard Reports*, 8 (1957): 208-310.
11. See Allison M. Martin and W.A. Lewis, "Patterns of Public Revenue and Expenditure," *Manchester School of Economic and Social Studies*, vol. 24, no. 3 (September 1936), pp. 203-244.
12. *Hansard Reports*, 2 (1962-1963): 416, 419.

There had, of course, been administrative measures to increase efficiency, such as those involving integration of the services concerned with revenue collection. Separate services had led to owners of lands and buildings making different evaluations for different tax assessments. For example, a property might be given high initial or depreciation allowances and low land and buildings taxes.

The first tax reform of legislative importance centered on the way income was charged to tax. The existing law followed the British method of basing taxes upon the income of the previous year, which evoked the taxpayer's criticism that his tax position was being altered on income already spent or committed. Consequently, a basis of up-to-date assessment was introduced. Taxpayers now estimate their income for the year, and whatever adjustments prove necessary are made during the succeeding year. The income of the preceding year was deemed to be the estimate for the current year's basis of assessment. The commissioner has latitude to vary the estimate, but only in the taxpayer's favor.

The second major reform was in the treatment of contributions to life insurance and to pension funds. Anyone purchasing life insurance after January 1, 1963, was allowed to deduct from chargeable income up to 40 percent of his insurance premium up to a maximum of $800 and up to one-sixth of his income in pension fund contributions. Self-employed people were previously allowed the same deductions for old age security and insurance as other persons were permitted for insurance only. The new law made provision for deducting contributions to deferred annuities. One effect of the new legislation was, understandably, an immediate spurt in pension plans of all sorts.

The third major reform was the treatment of covenants, or settlements as they were described in the amending legislation. Under the old law, a person could enter into a covenant to divest himself of his income for between two and three years. Through this allowance a person might avoid paying a tax on his taxable income by assigning it, say, to another member of his family in a lower tax bracket. That income was legally free of tax. The qualifying period was extended to six years, except for covenants favoring university students, charities, sporting organizations, and the like, in which cases the minimum period remained at two years. There were also provisions limiting convenants in favor of relatives or other persons in the employment of the taxpayer.

Restrictions were placed also on the expenses of business directors. Expenses not otherwise subject to tax under the amending law were treated as perquisites of office and regarded as emoluments. Borderline expenses were disallowed. The point here was that the taxpayer now bore the burden of proof. Finally, there was an upward adjustment in the rates to cover the costs of expanded services.

Among the more far-reaching changes in the law was a provision for a tax appeal board with a chairman having legal qualifications and appointed by the Judicial and Legal Service Commission.

Issues arising out of the amending legislation related to such matters as the complexity of the law, the basis of estimating income, dates for submission of returns, taxpayer setoffs against sums owed by the commissioner to the taxpayer, the meaning of "voluntary curtailment of business" as it related to tax avoidance, the special position of persons deriving their income from agriculture, the definition of settlements, and numerous other matters of detail.

A further amendment in 1964 made no great adjustments to the income tax law but served to tidy up the previous amendment by clarifying the language and removing doubts regarding interpretation.

No changes were introduced in the tax structure in 1965, but the 1965 budget speech gave indications of the government's thinking on further reforms, especially in the matters of separating individual and corporate taxes and taxing capital gains.

While tax and tariff reforms were being enacted, preparations were in progress for institutional reforms with emphasis on banking and insurance. These institutions had been the means of external financial control and the avenues by which savings had been channeled abroad in the past, bringing about the country's overdependence on foreign investment. It was these areas that the government had expected to hand over to federal control, and, perhaps as a consequence, they had received little attention prior to independence.

THE BANKING ACTS OF 1964

Transformation of the banking system came about through two legislative enactments—the Central Bank Act and the Commercial Banking Act, both passed in 1964. Both were presented to Parliament only after exhaustive preparation, which included consultation with monetary experts from the academic sector, officials of the International Monetary Fund (IMF), and central bankers from Italy, the United Kingdom, the United States, Japan, Iran, and Jamaica (where a central bank with limited powers had been established prior to Jamaica's attaining independence).

The Central Bank Act

The case for a central bank rested on the need for effective monetary management and the need to relate all aspects of finance to the long-range economic requirements of the country.

In presenting the bill for establishment of the central bank, the minister of finance made it clear how he expected the institution to be oriented:

It follows that whatever may be the traditional functions of a central bank in industrialised societies, the main function of a central bank in Trinidad and Tobago must be to assist in doing in the monetary field all such things as would promote development, primarily by producing conditions most conducive to the flow of long-term investment into the productive sectors of the economy. Credit policy should not encourage [the purchase of] motor cars and refrigerators at the expense of machinery, plant, and equipment, or at the expense of agriculture or housing. Portfolio management and reserve policies should not encourage the export of savings at the expense of domestic investment.[1]

The minister further pointed out the need, in pursuing the goal of economic development, to strike a balance between expansion and sta-

1. *Hansard Reports,* 4 (1964):280.

bility. It was necessary, therefore, as far as possible, to preserve a stable currency. Sensitivity to the local environment was a point he emphasized in presenting the bill:

It will do no good merely to transplant a central bank with the functions of the Bank of England or the Federal Reserve System of the United States or the Bundes Bank of [the Federal Republic of] Germany or the Bank of France or any of these banks which have developed their orientation and techniques in highly industrialised societies. It will do no good to apply these techniques and instruments uncritically to the circumstances of Trinidad and Tobago.[2]

The minister called for hard thinking on monetary problems, the application of knowledge gained from the experiences of other countries to the special circumstances of Trinidad and Tobago, and a staff of the highest possible caliber for the central bank.

The legislation provided for phasing the activities of the bank to keep it within the limitations of available personnel and enable other financial institutions to adjust to the new conditions. Thus arose the technique of passing an entire act but putting its components into effect at different times, rather than forcing it to undergo the hazards of periodic amendment.[3]

The legislation comprised the following nine sections: establishment, constitution, and management of the bank; currency and legal tender; capital and revenue; business of the bank; relations with other banks; relations with the government; accounts, reports, and statistics; miscellaneous provisions, and transitional provisions and repeal of existing legislation for the transition from currency board to central bank.

Negotiations to withdraw from the currency board were completed prior to the passing of the legislation, but the law empowered the board to continue issuing currency, as agent for the central bank, until the bank itself was ready to take over this function. The law also gave the bank the exclusive right to issue and redeem currency notes and coins in Trinidad and Tobago.

The act outlined the purpose of the bank as follows:

2. *Ibid.*, p. 281.
3. The method adopted had the advantage of clarifying from the start the proposed structure, purpose, and functions of the bank. It also reduced the opportunities for rallying opposition through frequent debates on specific items of legislation.

The bank shall have as its purpose: the promotion of such monetary, credit, and exchange conditions as are most favorable to the development of the economy of Trinidad and Tobago, and shall, without prejudice to the other provisions of this Act—

(a) have the exclusive right to issue and redeem currency notes and coins in Trinidad and Tobago;

(b) act as banker for, and render economic, financial, and monetary advice to the Government;

(c) maintain, influence, and regulate the volume and conditions of supply of credit and currency in the best interest of the economic life of Trinidad and Tobago;

(d) maintain monetary stability; control and protect the external value of the monetary unit; administer external monetary reserves; and encourage expansion in the general level of production, trade, and employment; and

(e) undertake continuously economic, financial, and monetary research.

Clearly, the bank was to be a dynamic institution in a dynamic environment as opposed to the traditional central bank and its preoccupation with monetary stability. The makeup of the bank's board of directors reflected its functions: a governor, appointed for not less than five years (except for the first governor, who was expected to be a foreigner),[4] a deputy governor, and four directors.

To ensure a fully independent bank, it is established by law as a corporation. Further, the governor and deputy governor are barred from other employment, whether paid or unapid, while they hold positions with the bank. The office of governor or deputy cannot be filled by a member of Parliament, a member of any municipal corporation or county council, a government employee, or a shareholder in any financial institution subject to regulation by the bank.

However, the governor or deputy governor may, with the approval of the minister of finance, serve on government committees inquiring into currency, banking, economic, and financial matters. They may also serve on international financial institutions or corporations in which the government or the bank has financial or other interests. The governor is answerable only to the board of directors for his acts and decisions but may be discharged for prescribed reasons of incapacity or misconduct.

To ensure coordination with official policies, the government ap-

4. The first governor was John F. Pierce of the United States. As it turned out, the second governor was also a foreigner, Alexander McLeod, of Canada. The first Trinidad and Tobago citizen to head the bank was Victor Bruce, who took office in 1969.

points all members of the board. One director must come from the treasury department and another from the agency responsible for economic planning. The minister of finance may, after consultation with the governor, issue general directives to effect current government monetary and fiscal policies. Though it is allowed latitude to operate with day-to-day efficiency, the bank must obtain ministerial approval in such specific matters as the following: salaries exceeding $12,000 per year; the bank's pension plan; denominations, forms, and designs of notes and coins; appointment of auditors; and purchase or lease of official residences.

The minister of finance put the bank's position in the following perspective:

The actual practice varies somewhat in different countries, but there is no doubt about the principle involved in this relationship. There has to be harmony and coordination between monetary, fiscal, and financial policies. Consequently, there has to be some authority which lays down the policy that has to be pursued by all these institutions. This does not mean that the policy will be arbitrarily laid down. It will be done on the basis of advice received after consultation. But after a decision has been made, there can be no question of any bickering or any struggle as to whether the policy should be pursued or not. There can be only one government in the country, and there can be only one Parliament and the Government is responsible to Parliament and the Parliament ultimately to the people. That principle has been appreciated in most countries, and certainly in those which have drawn the major part of their institutional background from the British model.[5]

Apart from the relationship between the bank and the government, there are other significant aspects of the central bank law. One such provision was the parity clause, which determined the parity of the Trinidad and Tobago dollar at four shillings and two pence sterling (approximately $0.58 United States currency at that time) or 0.518391 grams of fine gold. This provision aimed at stilling any apprehension regarding the stability of the currency after independence.[6] The act also contained a convertibility clause requiring the bank to issue on demand its notes and coins for immediate delivery in London in exchange

5. *Hansard Reports*, 4 (1964): 291.
6. As the currency of most formerly British territories is still closely tied to sterling, British devaluation in November 1967 required commensurate devaluation of all the currencies of such territories in the Caribbean. The Trinidad and Tobago dollar was also devalued. The Trinidad and Tobago dollar stood at approximately $0.50 United States currency as of July 31, 1970.

for the sterling equivalent and allowing the bank also to redeem its notes and coins for sterling. For this purpose the bank was empowered to fix the usual exchange charge, which is not to exceed 1 percent of the sum exchanged. The parity and convertibility clauses helped to smooth the transition to monetary independence, and will be amended as circumstances permit.

Another notable provision is the one dealing with the currency cover, which included, along with the usual forms of cover, contributions or advances to the capital of international financial organizations. Thus, Trinidad and Tobago's gold contributions to the IMF, our subscription to the World Bank and its sister institutions, our contribution to the Inter-American Development Bank and to the Caribbean Development Bank were all included in the 50 percent note cover required to be held in securities other than those of the government of Trinidad and Tobago.

Aside from the standard provisions regarding business procedures, the central bank has been given the rather unusual power to acquire, hold, and sell shares or other securities of any statutory body or any company registered under the Companies Ordinance in order to promote the development of a money or securities market or to finance economic development. The total holdings of such shares, however, may not exceed the bank's aggregate total of authorized capital and its general reserve fund.

Also significant are the provisions for selective credit controls and the cautious drafting of these provisions:

1. In order to determine what steps, if any, are necessary to be taken to encourage the expansion of credit in any or all sectors of the economy, the Bank shall from time to time consult with the commercial banks.
2. The Bank may, after consultation with the commercial banks, and with the approval of the Minister, impose controls in respect of the volume, terms, and conditions upon which credit may be made available to all or any sectors of the economy, when in its judgment the imposition of such controls is necessary to restrict or prevent an undue expansion of credit.
3. The imposition of any controls under the provisions of subsection (2) of this section shall be by notice published in the *Gazette*, and the provisions of any such notice shall take effect on or after the date of publication as may be stated in the notice and shall apply uniformly to all commercial banks.
4. The provisions of subsections (1), (2), and (3) shall apply mutatis

mutandis [the necessary changes having been made] to such financial institutions, persons, or classes of persons as may be designated by notice issued by the Minister to such financial institutions, persons, or classes of persons and published in the *Gazette*.[7]

The language of these sections reflected the desire to reassure the banking community in the face of strong objections to the powers being granted by the act.

The Commercial Banking Act

The Commercial Banking Act first requires the issue of a license to carry on banking. Every application must proceed through the central bank to the minister of finance, who, after consulting with the central bank, decides whether to grant or refuse a license. The application must include such particulars as the names of the applicants, the amount of authorized capital, the address of the registered office in Trinidad and Tobago, names and addresses of directors, a certified copy of the memorandum and articles of association, and an audited or certified copy of the organization's latest balance sheet. Other provisions regulate authorized, subscribed, and paid-up capital for both domestic and foreign companies.

Banks already doing business were allowed to obtain provisional licenses and given time to apply for a license and fulfill the various requirements of the act. Licenses are renewable annually upon satisfaction of licensing requirements and payment of a license fee. The minister of finance may revoke a license upon prescribed grounds of misconduct, and the bank has the right to appeal such a move. The act contains the usual restrictions as to who may act as directors or officers of a bank, and there are also restrictions upon such practices as a bank's acquiring or dealing in its own shares or offering credit facilities to its directors or other firms in which its directors or managers hold interests.

Other provisions regulate cash reserves, reserve funds, maximum liability requirements, and requirements for liquid assets ratios. The most significant provision is the requirement that in placing its liquid assets a bank should give preference to short-dated instruments originating in Trinidad and Tobago to further the government's goal of promoting an indigenous capital market.

7. To date, the bank has not yet made use of its power of selective credit control.

The provision creating an inspector of banks caused considerable objections on the grounds that the power of inspection, aside from being open to abuse, is unnecessary because the banks operating in Trinidad and Tobago were branches of large financial institutions of unquestionable integrity. In replying to such criticism, the minister of finance said:

But this is not an argument for keeping these provisions out of the law. Moreover, there is a lot of very useful statistical information which can be obtained by this means, and which will be very necessary. Consequently there is no reason whatsoever why these provisions should be omitted from the law. As a matter of fact, the banks are quite accustomed in all the countries in which they operate to have inspection. It is quite normal in countries which have made the transition from colonialism to independence that institutions which were subjected to no supervision whatsoever wish to continue in the same position in the newly independent countries, even though they are quite accustomed to supervision and even regulation and control in the metropolitan areas in which they operate.[8]

To still apprehensions over indiscreet or improper disclosure of confidential information, the act contains severe penalty clauses for such disclosures by either the inspector or members of his staff. Banks submit to the central bank a monthly statement of assets and liabilities, a quarterly analysis of loans and advances, and a yearly statement showing earnings and expenses. The act specifically provides, however, that no statement or return is to be required with respect to the affairs of individual customers of a bank. It is made clear that concern is to be with general statistical patterns rather than with isolated cases.

In presenting the bill to the House of Representatives, the minister of finance emphasized the new spirit of cooperation that already had appeared in anticipation of the act:

Already there are indications of a new relationship between the banking community and the interests of the community as a whole. Only today, as a result of changes which took place in the United Kingdom, and which in the ordinary circumstances would have resulted in automatic change in Trinidad and Tobago, consultation has already been initiated between the banks and the officers here for the establishment of the Central Bank, even though it has not yet come into operation, with a view to arriving at some sort of common outlook as to the measures which should be adopted in the circumstances in which we find ourselves as a result of the special measures being taken in the United Kingdom. This indicates already that there is a new spirit of co-opera-

8. *Hansard Reports*, 4 (1964):378.

tion. There ought to be from all these indications no reason why the new legislative framework should not be able to be the proper environment within which the interests of the public at large and the interests of the banking system could be harmonized, or at least co-ordinated in such a way as to result in the mutual benefit of these institutions and the public at large.[9]

THE BANKING ACTS IN PROCESS

Preparations for enactment of the banking bills took place simultaneously with arrangements for Trinidad and Tobago's withdrawal from the colonial currency board. The intricate nature of the matters required setting up a special secretariat in the Ministry of Finance to handle all monetary matters and also to expedite establishment of the central bank.

The discussions with officials of the International Monetary Fund were unexpectedly difficult. In the later stages, they even attempted to influence the actual drafting of the legislation. The officials selected for the purpose had little knowledge of the constitutional system of Trinidad and Tobago or of British legislative methods, which Trinidad and Tobago had used as models. Even with ministerial support, the Trinidad and Tobago draftsman had trying moments in resisting impositions by fund officials, obviously more used to dealing with Latin American matters.

After some two years of preparation, the bills were drafted and given restricted circulation within the business and banking community. Written comments were invited.

The two chief objections to the banking bills were that the central bank was an expensive luxury and that it was a dangerous instrument whose cutting edge should be blunted. The latter point was the chief complaint of the Trinidad Chamber of Commerce, which objected to the central bank's authority to regulate the operations of the commercial banks. The chamber summarized its position in a memorandum of July 9, 1964, part of which reads:

This country is fortunate—perhaps almost unique—in that its commercial banking business is in the hands of a number [six] of very substantial and long established international banks backed by huge resources. These banks have brought to Trinidad and Tobago the combined expe-

9. *Ibid.*, 4 (1966):380.

rience of British, Canadian, and North American banking practices and, although they are highly competitive with each other, they nevertheless conduct their business according to the strict banking disciplines practised in the United Kingdom and North America. The Chamber does not doubt for a moment that these banks, each of which has a substantial interest in this country, will be willing to co-operate to the full with the Central Bank both in the furnishing of statistical information regarding deposits, loans, liquid assets, reserves, and the like and in carrying out any policies the Central Bank might formulate in the furtherance of its objectives.

For this reason and also for the reason that it is doubtful whether it is possible, or advisable, to lay down a monetary policy with such precision as will render it enforceable at law, the Chamber strongly recommends that the most serious consideration be given to deferring the imposition of any formal controls of the type contemplated by these clauses until practical experience of voluntary co-operation by the commercial banks has shown what formal controls (if any) are required and the conditions on which such controls may be imposed.

It is well known that voluntary co-operation between the commercial banks and the Bank of England in the administration of the monetary policy formulated from time to time by the Bank of England has worked very well in the United Kingdom. Indeed, it is thought that the absence of any formal power in the Bank of England to exercise any legal control over the operations of U.K. commercial banks has largely contributed to the high degree of co-operation that exists between the Bank and the commercial banks. The commercial banks follow the policy recommendations of the Bank of England, not because they are legally forced to do so, but because they know that the latter's recommendations will be based upon sound economic and monetary policies. The Bank of England, in its turn, will take special care to frame its recommendations in accordance with sound banking practice in order to ensure their free acceptance by the commercial banks. . . .

For the above reasons, the Chamber strongly recommends the deletion of clauses 40-42 and 44 and the substitution therefor of a provision simply empowering the Central Bank to consult with the commercial banks on all matters concerning the volume and conditions of supply of credit and currency, the scale of deposits to be kept with the Central Bank from time to time, the proportion that the banks' Trinidad and Tobago assets should bear to their deposit liabilities in Trinidad and Tobago and other related matters, and from time to time to issue requests to the commercial banks regarding the monetary policies that the Central Bank desires the commercial banks to follow. The Central Bank should also be empowered to request the commercial banks to supply statistical information.[10]

10. Memorandum of the Trinidad Chamber of Commerce dated July 9, 1964, on the Draft Central Bank of Trinidad and Tobago Bill, 1964.

There were many other comments on specific sections of the draft bill, but this was the substance of the chamber's case. There were also comments from six commercial banks operating in Trinidad and Tobago: the Royal Bank of Canada, Barclays Bank, the Chase Manhattan Bank, the Bank of London and Montreal, the Bank of Nova Scotia, and the Canadian Imperial Bank of Commerce. All opposed the central bank's power to apply selective controls; they advocated "moral suasion" rather than legislative power.

Next came discussions with the representatives of these banks on the basis of the draft bill and the memoranda. Present as an observer at the discussions was John F. Pierce, one of the officials of the New York Federal Reserve Bank, who had been chosen to become the first governor of the central bank. During the three days of discussions it became clear that a major cause of fear among the managers of the branch banks arose from both their lack of experience at the policy level and a concomitant hesitancy to take action without specific instructions from their home offices. Wherever possible and appropriate, amendments were made to the draft to satisfy questions raised in the memoranda and during the discussions, but the essential ingredients of the banking bills were retained intact.

The next stage of the proceedings was the presentation of the bill in Parliament. By 1965, when Trinidad and Tobago established its own central bank, the institution had become common in almost every independent country, and there were numerous precedents to draw upon. However, there was little experience as to the effects of the central bank in less developed countries. As a result of some of the difficulties that had been recognized, especially in the area of staffing, the IMF later established a central banking advisory service. The service proved so effective that within three years no less than thirty newly independent countries had obtained its assistance, one of the more impressive achievements of the IMF.

During its first four years, however, Trinidad and Tobago's central bank, in contrast to the central bank of Iraq, for example, acted as hardly more than a currency board and made little impact on the domestic economic scene.

The conservatism of the institution was due largely to three factors: leadership remaining in the hands of a foreign governor and foreign advisers who were unacquainted with the local environment, the conservatism of the local banking and business community, and a board of directors largely without experience in the field of monetary policy. Consequently, the tendency was to do little rather than risk making mistakes. Even the limited expertise that the bank did acquire would not have accrued to it if it had followed the recruitment policy of the commercial banks, which the first governor of the bank had proposed. It was hardly a secret that in hiring personnel the commercial banks restricted their selection to a very small proportion of the population differentiated on ethnic lines. Had this practice become common to the central bank, it would doubtless have resulted in an inferior staff, especially in the fields of accountancy, law, and economics.

THE INSURANCE ACT, 1966

The need for regulation of the insurance business stemmed from two factors: its size and its practices. Its importance can be inferred from the fact that premiums from life insurance companies had risen from $9,821,000 in 1956 to $20,449,000 in 1963. Including premiums from other operations, the total premium income of the insurance business would have amounted to well over $30,000,000 by 1966. Moreover, insurance had developed into one of the principal channels for savings: by 1964 the assured value of life insurance policies alone had reached $566,000,000.

Virtually all insurance business was in the hands of foreign companies operating through local branches with local managers. Investment policies of these companies were, not surprisingly, attuned more to home office needs than to the interests of Trinidad and Tobago and its policyholders. Also, the business was attracting a growing number of companies and agents having no claim to and making no pretense of either business or ethical standards.

In one case a husband and wife decided to form an insurance company with an authorized capital of $250,000 divided into 25,000 shares at $10 each. At the outset total paid-up capital amounted to $75,000 by allotment of 7,500 shares at $10 each. After making the required deposit of $48,000, they retained the balance of $27,000 for use as working capital. During the first four months of operation of the business, the company issued approximately 350 insurance policies representing a coverage of $800,000.

In another case a company began business as a local private auto insurance company with two shareholders and an authorized capital of $100,000 made up of 100 shares at $1,000 each. Sixty shares were issued at $800 each, making up the required deposit of $48,000. The company collected installment premiums of $1,100 during the first eleven days of business and $5,327.51 more during the next thirty days. Each of the two directors received a salary of $400 a month, and each of five clerks received $100 a month. Overhead and operating expenses amounted to some $4,000 a month. The company's ploy was to deny liability for all claims. The standard tactic of this practice is that when the claim is made, the company states that it is communicating with its client, who has not yet reported the accident. Time passes,

7 INSURANCE REFORM

and in reply to inquiries the company states that the matter is under investigation and requests a detailed statement of the claim. On receipt of a reply, the company denies liability, and a lawsuit becomes the only recourse. By the time of the hearing in the courts, witnesses have often suffered loss of memory or died, or their testimony cannot stand up to cross-examination. Thus, many legitimate claims have been denied, with consequent loss and injustice to claimants and countless opportunities for malpractice on the part of insurance companies.

Not all the fault lay with the companies, though; they had, after all, developed their policies within the framework of existing law. The fact was that the insurance business as a whole was not pulling its weight in the light of national interests. Of the twenty-two life insurance companies doing business in Trinidad and Tobago, twelve paid no taxes in 1962; of the ten that did, two paid less than $100 each, and three paid between $1,000 and $5,000. In the same year the total premium income of these companies exceeded $20 million, and their investment income was over $4 million, yet they paid an aggregate tax bill of less than $250,000.

The weakness in the law was that a company could deduct all expenses whether incurred in acquiring premium income or investing it. Commissions on premiums and medical, management, and all other expenses were also deductible. The only income subject to taxation was investment income (the returns received from investment of the net premium income). The result of this arrangement was that many companies were successful enough to pay dividends of as much as 15 percent but never paid a penny in taxes.

Trinidad and Tobago's insurance law had been patterned after British insurance law. The latter, however, had undergone frequent amendment to keep pace with changing conditions. Moreover, in response to the pressure of public opinion, the British companies had evolved a fairly strict code of behavior, but parliamentary intervention had still been necessary from time to time. There had been little effort to modernize or strengthen the law in Trinidad and Tobago. It was, therefore, not only weak but obsolete as well.

Perhaps the fundamental difference was that companies operating in the United Kingdom were domestic; those same companies operating in Trinidad and Tobago were foreign and embodied all the classic characteristics of external control. The pattern was similar to that of banking but had led to greater abuses undoubtedly because of the greater opportunities for misconduct afforded by the nature of the business itself.

THE INSURANCE ACT IN PROCESS

The processing of the insurance act was similar to that of the banking acts. Apart from discussions with the local representatives of foreign firms, however, discussions also took place in London and Montreal. The companies doing business in Trinidad and Tobago were predominantly British and Canadian firms operating through local branches. Consequently the policies pursued by these companies, like those of the banks, were the offspring of the head offices in London and Montreal; Trinidad and Tobago agents were able merely to transmit communications. It was soon clear that a meaningful dialogue would be possible only by dealing directly with the principals.

It was, of course, feasible to invite them singly to Trinidad and Tobago to discuss matters, but the advantage of dealing with them collectively would have been lost. Moreover, the regulation of insurance business was only one part of the comprehensive program of transformation, and it seemed prudent to do everything reasonably possible to prevent the creation of a focal point for the forces of opposition.

Officials of the government indicated to representatives of the companies that the minister of finance would, on the occasion of his approaching visit to London and Montreal, welcome a meeting with insurance interests to discuss the insurance bill, and leaders of the respective organizations arranged the meetings.

The stock position of financial institutions that oppose reform legislation is that it is unnecessary. It was so with the banking bills, and it was so with the insurance bill. However, prior to the publication of the banking bills there had been only one bank failure in the history of the country, but there had been several insurance failures. Moreover, the undesirable practices that had crept into the business and the host of cases of claimants failing to obtain satisfaction were hardly secrets. It was not difficult, therefore, to obtain the concession that some kind of regulation was necessary. Once this principle was granted, the point at issue was precisely what the legislation should or should not contain.

The second position the companies took—again echoing the banking bills—was that whatever legislation ensued should be as simple as possible. The companies did not want to invest too much effort in filling out forms or interpreting the law. This objection was easy enough to meet in the case of officials of the North American companies, who were surprised at how well acquainted Trinidad and Tobago representatives were with the complexities of insurance legislation in Canada and the United States. It was also the issue on which Trinidad and Tobago could most easily make concessions, and several administrative provisions were deleted or modified accordingly.

The only two objects of the bill were to protect the policyholder and to assure investment in Trinidad and Tobago of a substantial portion of the premium income, which traditionally had been invested in the country of the home office. From the viewpoint of economic transformation, the second objective was much more important. Representatives of Trinidad and Tobago had to bear in mind constantly the ultimate objectives of the legislation.

The companies were well aware that the government placed high priority on local investment of a large proportion of premium income. Their first objection to this was that if such a condition applied in all the countries in which they did business, they could not possibly continue to manage their portfolios profitably. The reply of the Trinidad and Tobago representatives was that continuation of present investment practices would arrest the country's economic development and create social and political unrest and that the companies were subject to far more stringent investment requirements in their own countries.

Again, the justice of the principle was unassailable. It was not difficult to work out a formula acceptable to most of the companies, though not without several companies' threatening a complete cessation of business, an act of irresponsibility that had noticeably ill effects on the investment attitude toward Trinidad and Tobago.

Threats and lamentations notwithstanding, during the year after the passing of the act, no fewer than ten local and thirty-six foreign companies registered under its provisions. That same year these companies made deposits of $13 million,[1] or more than one-fifth of the financing required for the annual development program; several million dollars went into mortgages and other investments.

1. Trinidad and Tobago, Supervisor of Insurance, *Annual Report,* 1967.

PROVISIONS OF THE INSURANCE ACT

The 1966 insurance act first required registration of all companies wishing to do business in Trinidad and Tobago; a primary prerequisite of registration was either incorporation or a place of business within Trinidad and Tobago. For local companies doing long-term (mainly life insurance) business, the act requires a minimum paid-up share capital; for mutual companies, a minimum uncommitted reserve of $250,000. The act demands of a foreign company doing long-term business a deposit of the same amount.

An auto insurance company, local or foreign, must also make a deposit of $250,000 or 40 percent of its premium income, whichever is greater. Premium income is calculated on the basis of the income of the previous financial year as certified by a chartered accountant. Insurance companies other than those doing long-term or motor vehicle insurance business must make a deposit of $100,000 or 40 percent of the premium income, whichever is the greater. In each case, the deposit must be in cash or approved securities.

A major provision of the act requires that a company carrying on long-term insurance business must place in trust (in Trinidad and Tobago) assets equal to the liabilities and the contingency reserve of Trinidad and Tobago policyholders. To meet objections that assets would be frozen in case of an absence of a capital market in Trinidad and Tobago, the act provides that with the approval of the minister assets may be held in London, Ottawa, or Washington. This provision also applies to auto insurance companies, but with the stipulation that assets held in the statutory fund must equal liabilities and reserve less the amount held on deposit.

Another provision requires a local assets ratio of 60 percent of the total premium income but allows a minimum grace period of five years to achieve it. To halt the improper conduct so prevalent in the auto insurance business, other provisions regulate accounting, balance sheets, and audit procedures.

The administrative key to the insurance act was the establishment of a supervisor of insurance and an insurance department within the Ministry of Finance. The minister of finance must furnish the supervisor with the services of an actuary if the supervisor is not himself an actuary. The supervisor must submit to Parliament annual reports on the effectiveness of the act. Finally, he has the power to delegate his functions, to arbitrate disputes between company and policyholder, and—perhaps most significant—to investigate companies suspected of improper conduct. Regarding the last function, the act includes severe penalties for unauthorized disclosure of information.

The act also contains rigorous requirements to expedite judicial action (especially in cases formerly subject to lengthy probate) and provides automatic paid-up status for defaulted policies, strict administration and investment of pensions funds, and penalties for fraud and misrepresentation by agents and companies.

In assessing the often parochial objections to the banking and insurance acts, it is necessary to bear in mind that the basic cause of uneasiness was the very fundamental change that the acts were about to cause in the banking and insurance systems themselves. The banking system had evolved in a colonial economy that emphasized the export of primary products. Preference was given to commercial enterprises, particularly those with a foreign exchange bias. The effect in currency and banking was to promote the neglect of indigenous industry and agriculture other than export crops and concentrate on primary products—sugar, citrus, and oil—and in any other area with a strong foreign exchange content. Moreover, banking and insurance policies were determined by head offices on the basis of financial conditions in the home country, which caused immediate and certainly not always favorable reactions in the colonies.

The transfer of political power and the adoption of a concrete program of development required the liquidation of a whole system, of which banking and insurance were key parts.

Some of the apprehensions about changing the banking and insurance businesses were, of course, justified; most of them, though, have proved to have been nothing more than fears of the unfamiliar and untried. And for a nation that balks at ventures simply because they are unfamiliar, there can be no genuine independence.

The Finance Act of 1966 marked the culmination of reform in direct taxation. Along with the reforms of 1962 and 1963 in the field of indirect taxation, it formed the guidelines of the country's tax structure in the era of independence.

The chief objectives of the bill were as follows:

1. To improve the administration and efficiency of tax collection and provide better means of satisfying taxpayers' complaints.

2. To minimize tax evasion.

3. To collect taxes in money then being unjustifiably diverted to foreign countries.

4. To lower the taxes of skilled and professional employees.

5. To achieve a system of taxing profits appropriate to the country's needs.

6. To remove the inducements to distribution and consumption and replace them with incentives to reinvestment.

7. To offer incentives for the expansion of productive employment and exports.

8. To introduce a tax on capital gains formerly untaxed or evaded.

9. To provide for relief from double taxation.

THE CASE FOR REFORM

International Background

The finance act was conceived and passed during a period of considerable world pressure on sterling. Prior to this time the dollar had been encountering such difficulty that the United States introduced measures to reduce capital outflow. Most developing countries were exempt from them, but the general climate the measures tended to bring about affected them adversely, and the United Kingdom compounded the difficulty by applying its own measures to defend the pound. A further measure adopted by these and other developed countries to defend their balance of payments was to encourage overseas branches of metropolitan-based firms to repatriate all possible profits and to move even working balances to metropolitan centers.

The general international financial situation in 1966 was that terms of trade had for some time been moving consistently to the disadvantage of the less developed countries, partly because of rapidly rising prices of needed manufactured goods unavailable except through imports. More-over, substantial increases in interest rates had made borrowing diffi-cult. What international economic and financial aid there was had a number of strings attached to it, such as the one requiring that the aid money be spent in the donor country. In addition, there was an in-crease in the indebtedness of the poor nations to the rich, and existing double taxation treaties also favored the developed countries.

Trinidad and Tobago was particularly vulnerable to the consequences of these measures, as foreign companies accounted for about 85 percent of profits subject to the country's tax laws. The condition highlighted not only the danger of potential capital outflow but also the unsuitable nature of the entire prevailing tax system. Because of this situation, it was but a small step to the ideas of separation of personal income tax from corporate tax and the introduction of a withholding tax. Actually, most company profits arising in Trinidad and Tobago were already sub-ject to a corporation tax since nonresidents could not resort to the "grossing-up" provisions that were available to those holding Trinidad and Tobago residency.

Under the earlier system, businesses paid taxes at the 42.5 percent company rate. A dividend recipient, however, paid personal taxes on those dividends only if his personal tax rate exceeded the company rate. If the company rate exceeded the personal tax rate, the Inland Revenue refunded the difference. The procedure for computing the tax rate was known as "grossing up."

As for this grossing-up procedure, offering a tax advantage to resident dividend recipients could be of advantage to Trinidad and Tobago only as long as countries that made up its major sources of foreign capital also retained this kind of system. This had long since ceased to be the case with the United States, which had recently become Trinidad and Tobago's major trading partner and source of investment capital; Can-ada, in a similar position, had adopted the corporation tax system. Finally, the United Kingdom, second only to the United States in trade and as a source of investment capital, had also made the transition—co-incidentally, at the same time as Trinidad and Tobago, though neither country was aware that the other was considering such action. Since tax levels in all of these countries were higher than in Trinidad and Tobago, tax uncollected in Trinidad and Tobago actually accrued to them.

The existing system of corporate law and tax treatment had resulted in a plethora of private companies being used, among other things, as means of minimizing individual tax liability. Of 567 resident companies in 1964, 547 were private. All of the country's 640 registered firms, which includes foreign companies, together paid a total of only $50 million in income tax, and 95 percent of it came from 25 percent of those companies.

The defects of the corporate structure had other fiscal implications; the social and political consequences were tight control of the economy of the country by an oligarchy made all the more limited through inter-locking directorships. The government would have found it increasingly difficult to promote national economic development under a system of concessions that fostered such a structure.

Subsidiary companies that distributed profits to parent firms in the United States created a special complication. Classified as western hemisphere companies, they enjoyed a preferential corporate tax rate of 34 percent, which was 14 percent below the normal rate. However, an examination of the companies that tax changes might affect showed that concessions apart from the hemispheric allowances put these companies in an even lower effective tax bracket.

A major difficulty arose from companies operating from tax-haven countries. Without conceding the case for special tax treatment of such companies, there was general agreement to reduce the statutory rate even in cases of countries with which there was no double taxation treaty if it appeared useful to do so.

Another curious feature of the previous legislation was the provision that unearned income was taxable wherever it arose, but earned income was not taxed unless received in or brought into Trinidad and Tobago. A professional person, for example, could earn fees abroad and not have to pay tax on them as long as he did not bring them into the country.

THE FINANCE BILL IN PROCESS
The principal objectives of the bill were officially announced in the minister of finance's budget speech to the House of Representatives on January 15, 1965. More detailed proposals were announced several

months later. Still later, a draft bill was circulated for comment, first to business interests and then to the general public.

Reaction was negative from the start. The principal objection was to separate tax treatment for companies and individuals. The Trinidad and Tobago Association of Chartered Accountants and Certified Accountants commented, "Although there is adequate precedent in fully developed economies for the introduction of a Corporation Tax, we are of the opinion that its introduction in Trinidad at this stage of the country's development would adversely affect the growth of the economy."[1]

The Southern Trinidad Chamber of Industry and Commerce, on the other hand, felt that although the measure might simplify tax administration, "It will mean either a very substantial increase in the tax collected by Government if companies maintain their present net rate of dividend or it will mean a drastic reduction in the dividents declared by companies."[2]

The Southern Chamber of Commerce recommended a reduction in the corporate tax rate from the proposed figure of between 41 and 44 percent to between 28 and 30 percent.[3] The Trinidad Chamber of Commerce (not to be confused with the Southern Chamber of Commerce) stated that "The new tax proposals will completely upset all the accepted principles of taxation on which the whole financial and business structure of the country has been built up."[4] The chamber commented that the effects of the transition would

(a) Destroy the image of local companies.
(b) Defeat the incentives to investment in Trinidad companies.
(c) Inhibit local investors against corporate structures.
(d) Discourage investment from abroad.

Moreover, our examination of the information available to us shows that the detriments to which we have referred arise not only from the proposed rates given in the Budget Speech but from the change in the basic principles of taxation. A reduction in the rates of taxation whilst giving some relief will not, in our opinion, make for a more favorable

1. Memorandum to the minister of finance dated April 1, 1965.
2. Memorandum to the minister of finance dated February 23, 1965.
3. A fiscal review committee consisting of representatives of government, business, and labor subsequently recommended an increase in the corporation tax rate to 45 percent.
4. See *Trinidad Guardian* of February 13, 1966.

climate for the much needed investment from abroad or give the equally necessary impetus to the generation of local capital.[5]

In the face of such opposition, there had to be a decision as to whether to proceed to the stage of a draft law. Since the processing of the banking and insurance bills had shown the value of dialogue, the government decided to discuss matters with representatives of business and professional organizations. However, because those groups had asked for further details, it seemed wise to have something as specific as possible to discuss.

Accordingly, the Ministry of Finance prepared a draft bill and submitted it to the cabinet, which referred it to the cabinet's finance committee. After corrections and amendments, the cabinet released the draft to business groups and later to the public. The instrument was printed not as a bill but simply as a draft bill.

Its publication produced an immediate wave of criticism from leading business organizations, which called for its unconditional withdrawal.[6] The newspapers, radio, and television served as sounding boards for the mounting complaints. The South Trinidad Chamber of Industry and Commerce demanded the withdrawal of the bill. The chamber claimed in a memorandum to the finance minister:

Since your Speech last year, in which you intimated that you intended to adopt a Corporations Tax, the level of new investment has decreased and particularly since it became known that many of the proposals contained in the Preliminary Draft Bill under review would have a most adverse effect on investment. Indeed, it has come to our notice that a number of persons have already disposed of their existing investments and it is possible that they may now be dissuaded from considering reinvesting in Trinidad and Tobago. In our opinion the ultimate effect of the proposals in the Preliminary Draft Bill will be the closing of the door to new investment in Trinidad and Tobago. It is possible also that the Bill may encourage the conversion of many existing investments into a negotiable form, and these funds will then leave the country.[7]

The memorandum appeared over the signature of the president of the chamber, a manager of Barclay's Bank, the principal British banking institution in the country.

5. *Ibid.*
6. Even the president of the Trade Union Congress, W. W. Sutton, announced at a dinner given by the Trinidad Chamber of Commerce that he was in favor of the bill being withdrawn.
7. Memorandum to the minister of finance dated March 3, 1966.

In reply to such criticism, the minister of finance stated:

I think it would be absolutely foolish on the part of any person, let alone any person with any degree of responsibility, to suggest that it is not of great importance to Trinidad and Tobago that there should continue to be inflows of foreign capital and also re-investment of profits arising from enterprises controlled abroad and operating in Trinidad and Tobago. It would be absolute folly to suggest otherwise. But it would be even greater folly not to recognize the importance of domestic investment, and equally greater folly not to recognize the risks to which you are subject and the potentials of a situation in which 85 percent of your chargeable profits accrue to foreign companies: risks in respect of the balance of payments, risks in respect of the pressure which can be exercised on the government and on persons in administrative positions.[8]

The Trinidad Manufacturers' Association predicted that the proposals would increase the proportion of national income going to government as taxes and reduce the remaining disposable income and thereby depress the economy, lowering both disposable income and government revenue.[9]

The Trinidad Group of Incorporated Secretaries proposed an increase in duties and a purchase tax as alternatives to the corporate tax or a temporary tax increase "to tide the country over its present commitments."[10] All who submitted memoranda ignored the effect of double taxation treaties in calculating their increased liability, producing examples such as those shown in Table 8.1. The calculation takes into account the full 30 percent withholding tax but ignores proposed treaty rates varying from 15 percent to 5 percent. It also ignores, in the case of a foreign-based company, liability to tax on the same income in the firm's home country.

Faced with the staggering resistance, the minister of finance publicly restated that the government's purpose in publishing the bill for public comment prior to its introduction into Parliament was to allow discussion of the proposal, as had been the case with the banking and the insurance bills. He further indicated the government's willingness to make reasonable and proper changes in the legislation.

After the ministry of finance had the opportunity to examine the many criticisms, it began discussions with various organizations. Those

8. *Hansard Reports,* 7 (1966):1288.
9. Memorandum to the minister of finance dated March 30, 1966.
10. Memorandum to the minister of finance dated March 31, 1966.

Table 8.1. Example of Calculations Showing Effect of Proposed Taxes

	Present System	Proposed System
Profits before tax	$1,000	$1,000
Income tax	425	—
Corporation tax	—	440
	575	560
Withholding tax	—	168
Profits after Trinidad tax	$ 575	$ 392

Result: A reduction of 31.8 percent in profits after the proposed tax.

with the Trinidad Chamber of Commerce were proceeding fruitfully enough; then the chamber's representatives broke their commitment to meet with the minister of finance. It was soon clear that a determined campaign was underway to break off discussions and cause the withdrawal of the entire draft bill. In response to the demand for withdrawal, the prime minister set up and presided over a cabinet committee to consider the entire matter. The finance minister, without benefit of full discussions with the business community, then made his final recommendations to the committee.

Parliament passed the Finance Act of 1966 on September 27 of that year. The house deleted or modified some passages but retained all the essential features of the draft bill. It had proved to be an extremely difficult piece of engineering marked by highly organized opposition and heated controversy. Most disturbing perhaps was the successful campaign to break off the dialogue between government and business, among whom rapport, once ruptured, is exceedingly hard to restore.

PROVISIONS OF THE FINANCE ACT

Insurance
This provision requires that sums due on insurance policies qualifying for deductions from chargeable income should on maturity be payable in Trinidad and Tobago currency. Its aim was to meet the objections of insurance companies opposed to the provisions of the new insurance act setting minimum investment ratios in Trinidad and Tobago. During dis-

cussions on the insurance bill, insurance companies had argued that as monies due on their policies in the United States or Britain were payable in dollars or sterling, they had to maintain assets in the United States and the United Kingdom and would find it difficult to meet the minimum investment ratios.

Earned and Unearned Income

This provision was altered so that both earned and unearned income, wherever it arose, received equal treatment. The act established two important new principles: first, that all income arising within Trinidad and Tobago was subject to tax; and, second, that all income of residents of Trinidad and Tobago, wherever it arose, was also subject to tax. These two elements laid the foundations for subsequent treaty negotiations.

The Investment Company

To liberalize the corporate structure, the act introduced the concept of affording the investment company special tax treatment. The act defined an investment company as a resident company that within a year satisfies these conditions with respect to income:

(a) 100 per cent of the assets thereof are situated in Trinidad and Tobago;
(b) at least 80 per cent of its property owned throughout the year was shares, bonds, or marketable securities;
(c) not less than 90 per cent of its profits was derived from shares, bonds, or marketable securities;
(d) not more than 50 per cent of its gross revenue for the year was from interest;
(e) at no time in the year did more than 10 per cent of its property consist of shares, bonds, or marketable securities of any one company or debtor, other than those of the Government;
(f) at no time in the year was the number of shareholders of the company less than fifty, none of whom at any time in the year held more than 25 per cent of the shares or the capital stock of the company;
(g) 90 per cent or more of its profits (other than dividends or interest received in the form of shares, bonds, or other securities that had not been sold before the end of the year of income) was distributed to its shareholders within six months following the end of the accounting period for that year of income.[11]

The investment company requirements were designed along the lines of the "unit trust" in the hope that it would facilitiate public participation in the investment projects and equity capital of industrial compa-

11. Finance Act, Trinidad and Tobago, no. 42 of 1966, section 46 (3).

nies. For this reason the act declared the profits of the company tax-free. At the same time the government made it clear that in view of the novelty of this institution to Trinidad and Tobago, any proposals for genuine improvement would be welcome. To date (1970), however, no one has either established such a company or offered modifications to the act.

A related provision sought to remedy a deficiency in the treatment of initial allowances in the legislation of 1963. To facilitate the transition to the current basis of assessment, profits for that year were to be free of income tax. The intention had been that, with the freeing of profits from tax, allowances that would have been permissible against taxable profits of that year should not be carried forward to be deducted from profits of subsequent years. However, there was doubt regarding the legality of the provision, with the consequence that some $6 million was in danger of being lost to the treasury. The 1966 provision, severely criticized on the ground of "retroactivity," ensured the payment of the money.

Employment Allowance

This allowance was to be an incentive to increased employment and called for a straight tax reduction for every man-day of employment generated. The government withdrew it from the act because of the administrative complications it entailed.[12]

Export Allowance

Any company exporting products other than those specifically excluded (petroleum and sugar) is entitled to an export allowance. This allowance, which was increased in 1968, permitted a tax deduction of 1 percent from taxable profits from exports for every 1 percent of increase in export sales during the last three income years, provided that the allowance for any year did not exceed 44 percent of the taxable profits from exports. To assist new export companies, the act provided that if a company had made no export sales during its last three income years, it received the full 44 percent allowance.

Excluded from the allowance were reexports, sugar, petroleum and

12. After this proposal appeared in the 1966 budget, Britain's chancellor of the exchequer proposed an employment tax, the essence of which was precisely the reverse of that in Trinidad and Tobago, namely, to minimize the employment of labor in certain industries. The aim, however, was in both cases to influence aggregate employment in the economy.

petroleum products, pioneer industry products, and any other products that might be specified by the governor-general. Sugar and petroleum were excluded because they were already dominant, and the economy needed diversification. The allowance precluded attempts to benefit by deliberately reducing exports in one year to show an increase in a subsequent year. Pioneer companies were excluded because they already enjoyed tax exemptions and duty-free imports of plant, equipment, and raw materials.

Dividend Income Allowance

This allowance stemmed directly from separating individual from corporate tax, which, without such a provision as the dividend income allowance, could have adversely affected the return on domestic equity investment, at least in the short run. The allowance provided was an extremely liberal one in that dividends actually received were calculated to be the equivalent of 170 percent, 70 percent of which is tax-deductible. This provision restored as much as 95 percent of the excess burden that the resident shareholder of a resident company would otherwise have had to bear in consequence of the separation of individual from corporate taxes.

Taxation of Short-Term Capital Gains

Prior to the finance act, there had been no provision for the taxation of capital gains. The result, naturally, was widespread manipulation of income to give it the appearance of capital gain. The finance act sought to minimize this practice, especially that of a speculative nature. Short-term gains are described as chargeable gains accruing from disposal of an asset within twelve months of acquisition. Along with taking gains into account, the act declares losses on such transactions to be tax-deductible.

Certain transactions are exempt from the tax, the principal one being the marketing of local securities. Others include prizes from games and lotteries, currency acquired for personal expenditure outside Trinidad and Tobago, legal compensation or damages, private automobiles, household goods, and owner-occupied houses sold for less than $5,000.

On this occasion, as in 1963, the final version of the act was a simplified one containing what could be regarded as essential provisions from the revenue standpoint and designed to promote smooth progress toward economic transformation and development.

TREATIES TO PREVENT DOUBLE TAXATION

Certain sections of the finance act altering the tax position of foreign residents and firms allowed new treaties to be drawn up with the home countries of those residents and firms to prevent their being taxed twice on the same income. Several months prior to passage of the finance act, Trinidad and Tobago gave six months' public notice that it was withdrawing from existing treaties. These treaties had been drawn up between the United Kingdom and her major trading partners, colonies, and commonwealth members.

The first country the government approached for the purpose of drawing up new treaties was the United States, which was receiving by far the largest portion of the remittances from Trinidad and Tobago. Diplomatic channels provided preliminary contacts, and the stage was set for the opening of direct negotiations. Leading the United States team was Undersecretary of the Treasury Stanley Surrey, whose writings on double taxation treaties were well known to members of the Trinidad and Tobago negotiating team. For purposes of strategy, it was decided that the minister of finance make an opening statement and then withdraw from the discussions, leaving the actual negotiations to officials of the Ministry of Finance and the Department of Inland Revenue.

United States Treasury officials were aware of the difficulties besetting the draft bill; in fact, they initially took the stand that it would serve no useful purpose to negotiate a treaty on the basis of a bill that they understood would not go through because of a split in the cabinet. Trinidad and Tobago representatives replied that they were only civil servants and were concerned only with the negotiations, which the cabinet had approved. The United States officials then agreed to begin negotiations, which turned out to be difficult and lengthy. The Ministry of Finance had its hands full in resisting the pressures of not only international vested interests but domestic ones as well; ironically, both were pushing against the Ministry and in the same direction. The idea soon occurred to the negotiators that it might be easier to establish ground rules with one of the firms operating in Trinidad and Tobago. Texaco was the choice, and in many ways the discussions with Texaco were crucial to passing the finance act and the successful negotiation or partial negotiation of the double taxation treaties.

The dialogue with Texaco was opened at the highest level and was continued on an expert level. Although both parties were fully aware that the discussions were simply to ascertain the implications of proposals and objections and that they were in no sense formal negotiations, a breakdown in these discussions might well have doomed the finance bill and everything it represented. Texaco's attitudes, in sharp contrast to those of domestic business interests, were coldly logical and expert.

The major issue was the extent to which Trinidad and Tobago could win terms in harmony with its needs. Most existing treaties were based on the OECD (Organization for Economic Cooperation and Development) model worked out between developed countries, which normally had few problems with massive outflows and inflows of capital. To them it mattered little whether taxation was in the country of source or the country of residence so long as uniform principles applied. To the less developed country with a high proportion of foreign investment, such as Trinidad and Tobago, it is of great importance to obtain acceptance of the principle of taxation at source. For this purpose, much hinged on a modification of the definition in OECD treaties of the term "permanent establishment."

In these treaties, the standard definition includes a place of management, a branch, an office, a factory or workshop, a mine, quarry, or other place of extraction of natural resources, a building site, or a construction or assembly project that exists for more than twelve months. Usually excluded are such areas as places for storage, delivery, display of other enterprises, and areas for purchasing, collecting, or supplying information, advertising, scientific research, or similar activities of a preparatory or auxiliary character. Not included are operations of agents or visiting personnel and operations of a more temporary nature, which, as the Trinidad and Tobago delegation pointed out, would become increasingly prevalent with rapidly improving communications. On the basis of the argument, a much broader definition was accepted.

Also of importance to Trinidad and Tobago was the source of income rules. The first proposal of Trinidad and Tobago was that a nonresident corporation should remain liable to tax on distributed dividends, provided it earned 85 percent of its income within the taxing state. It also was proposed that the term "distributions" should replace "dividends."

Another objective was to obtain the benefit of the 7.5 percent tax deduction on business invesment that United States domestic corporations enjoyed, which by treaty had sometimes extended to overseas corporations or their branches. United States authorities were willing to grant the credit, but it was at the time under suspension by executive order to combat inflationary trends. Other points included the treatment of interests, rents, royalties, and management charges. The objective, though, was always to retain for the treasury of Trinidad and Tobago as much as possible of locally arising income without increasing the aggregate tax liability of the nonresident taxpayer.

Similar negotiations were conducted with the British and Canadian governments. Most difficult of all were the discussions with the United Kingdom, which reflected the stringent measures it was taking to minimize capital outflows and correct the unfavorable balance of payments. British authorities were very reluctant to grant "tax-sparing" facilities, the equivalent of the 7.5 percent investment credit. The United Kingdom's price for tax-sparing was freeing taxes on considerable areas of income arising in Trinidad and Tobago.

Negotiations with Canada and the Scandinavian countries were the least onerous. Concessions difficult to obtain from the United States and Great Britain were readily granted by the Scandinavian countries, perhaps partly because these countries had less equity in the matters, but also because they have been traditionally more flexible in their policies toward the developing nations. The chief of these concessions were provisions for tax-sparing and taxation at the source. In general, the experience with the Scandinavian countries was that once there was agreement on basic principles for the negotiations, it was not difficult to fit the technical details into the philosophical base of the discussions. Agreements on basic principles with U.S. authorities had a tendency to be eroded in working out the technical agreements, but U.K. authorities would not even agree to the basic principle of taxation at source. Finally, the unfavorable position that Trinidad and Tobago was seeking to redress in these negotiations was made even more difficult by the domestic political situation. It was the exceptional diligence and tenacity of the entire negotiating team that produced the series of agreements comprehensive enough to assure passage of the Finance Act of 1966, whose defeat or watering down would have meant, at the very least, a temporary cessation of reform.

THE NEED FOR ECONOMY

Along with fiscal and institutional reforms, measures were necessary to increase the efficiency and control the expenditures of government departments, with the major objective of achieving surpluses to finance economic development. Spending habits of the various departments had established themselves over the decade before independence in a climate of extraordinary expansion in the entire economy. However, the surplus of revenue over expenditures, a feature that had characterized the period from 1957 to 1961, had ceased to exist by the time of independence. Expenditures were rising faster than current revenue, and by 1962 existing taxes were wholly inadequate to finance recurrent expenditure.

Independence itself inevitably brought increased demands and expectations, and with the sharp decline in the growth rate, the necessity to apply restrictive measures could hardly have arisen at a more unfavorable time. In fact, the confluence of contrary forces at this time produced a critical period in the country's history.

The 1964 budget laid great emphasis on financial discipline:

Financial discipline means, firstly, a fiscal structure designed to raise adequate revenues to enable the Government to discharge its functions. It means, secondly, the collection of those revenues. Thirdly, it means the rigid control of expenditures. Fourthly, it means the proper appropriation of those expenditures. Fifthly, it means the relation of those expenditures to pre-determined ends based upon a rational order of priorities in accordance with the economic objectives and social and political philosophy of the government. Lastly, financial discipline means financial planning; and the essence of financial planning is so to manage the nation's finances that, on the one hand, the most effective use can be made of existing financial resources and, on the other . . . the maximum amount of additional reserves can be attracted. This requires a balance between immediate and pressing needs and long-term requirements.[1]

Capital expenditure over the period of the 1958-1962 development plan rose rapidly, while the current account surplus declined equally fast. The trend is illustrated in Table 9.1.

In 1962 current expenditure, in the absence of revenue measures, was expected to exhaust the current surplus entirely, which, if expenditures arising from independence are taken into account, would result in a deficit on current account of about $8 million.

1. *Hansard Reports*, 3 (1963-1964):719

BUDGET REFORM 9

Table 9.1. Capital Expenditure and Current Surplus, 1958-1961 (in millions)

Year	Current Surplus	Capital Expenditure	Overall Deficit
1958	$34.2	$37.0	$ 2.8
1959	28.0	29.5	1.5
1960	29.8	37.4	7.6
1961	5.3	61.7	56.4

Source: *Financial Statistics, 1967/1968*, Trinidad and Tobago: Central Statistical Office, Table 3, pp. 2-3.

SUSPENSION OF EXPENDITURES

The first step toward the improvement of financial administration was to require treasury approval to spend appropriations in each of the major spending ministries—health and housing, education, and public works. The treasury employed the power conferred on it by Parliament to suspend any outlay until it was satisfied that the expenditure was of sufficiently high priority. This was a drastic measure, but it ensured a continuing dialogue between the treasury and the ministries, regular supervision of expenditures, and a greater sense of financial responsibility at all levels.

SUPPLEMENTARY PERSONNEL APPROPRIATIONS

Prior to 1963 supplementary appropriations had been employed simply to obtain parliamentary approval for increased expenditures. Consequently, expenditure appropriations were increased frequently during the course of the year. In spite of an often obvious inability to spend the total increases, additions to appropriations for sorely needed personnel increases were no more likely to receive attention than those in which it was obvious that the money could not be spent. This practice, which had become entrenched over the years, had a highly inflationary effect on expenditures.

Since 1963 supplementary appropriations have been made almost exclusively for the purpose of transferring funds to areas that have the technical and organizational capacity to disburse them.

Table 9.2 demonstrates the effect of this measure by comparing the margin of error in expenditure estimates between 1953 and 1963. The greatest difficulty was with development program expenditures, in

Table 9.2. Supplementary Appropriations and Expenditure Estimates

Year	Percent of Error in Expenditure Estimate
1953	11.0
1954	15.0
1955	13.0
1956	14.0
1957	11.6
1958	12.0
1959	13.5
1960	13.0
1961	10.4
1962	10.8
1963	2.0

Source: *Hansard Reports*, 3 (1963-1964):711.

Table 9.3. Development Expenditure Estimates

Year	Estimate of Expenditure (in millions)	Actual Expenditure (in millions)	Percent of Error in Estimate
1958	$44.0	$28.4	35
1959	50.8	38.2	25
1960	65.0	38.6	41
1961	70.0	52.6	25
1962	82.0	60.7	26
1963	68.4	63.2	8

Source: *Hansard Reports*, 3 (1963-1964):713.

which shortfalls had been chronic, as Table 9.3 demonstrates.

It is clear that a major problem in the development plan was the capacity of the various ministries to spend their allocations effectively. The key to improvement was more a matter of organizing the departments than controlling the expenditure.

MISCONDUCT PENALTIES

Measures were also taken to ensure the proper use of funds once appropriated. The power to surcharge was already a part of earlier legislation but had never been used. The government made it clear, by notification placed in public offices, that it would use this power under section 31, subsections 1 and 2, of the Exchequer and Audit Ordinance, which read:

(1) If it appears to the Minister [of Finance] that any person who is or was in the employment of the Government
(a) has failed to collect any moneys owing to the Government for the collection of which he is or was responsible; or
(b) is or was responsible for any improper payment of public moneys or for any payment of such moneys which is not duly vouched; or
(c) is or was responsible for any deficiency in, or for the destruction of any public moneys, stamps, securities, stores, or other Government property;
and if a satisfactory explanation is not, within a period specified by him, furnished to the Minister with regard to such failure to collect, improper payment, payment not duly vouched, deficiency or destruction, the Minister may surcharge against the said person the amount of any such amount not collected, payment deficiency or loss or the value of the property destroyed as the case may be.
(2) The amount of any such surcharge made under this section, shall, subject to the provisions of section 33 of this Ordinance, be a debt due to Government from the person against whom the surcharge is made.

The power is an extremely far-reaching one but with the other measures forms a comprehensive program to instill in public officials a sense of financial responsibility.

SALARIES AND GRANTS

One of the three principal areas in the program to effect public economies was personal emoluments. Between 1955 and 1965 appropriations for personal salaries had produced persistent shortfalls ranging from 8 to 15 percent.

The consequences were twofold and in both cases had an inflationary effect on expenditures. First, some departments, anticipating shortfalls on such appropriations, sought to increase their budgets to undertake expenditures unanticipated in the original appropriation by stating that the funding for such expenditures was already available in the form of savings on personal emoluments. Second, a number of departments were unaware of what posts in their establishments were unfilled; some requested additional posts identical to already existing ones that they had been unable to fill; and many requested posts that, from past experience, they knew they had no prospect of filling. There were few attempts to redeploy existing staff to conform to realities.

The technique that the Ministry of Finance employed to rectify this situation was first to suspend expenditures for two months on all posts that remained unfilled by the date of suspension. Departments requiring vacancies to be filled or new posts to be created were required to send with their requests a statement of all unfilled posts, the period over which they had remained unfilled, and an appropriate order of priorities for filling them. The organization and methods division of the Ministry of Finance reviewed the requests and made appropriate recommendations to the cabinet, which included all ministers. Until the cabinet acted, no post could be filled without the specific approval of the Ministry of Finance.

The second area identified for action was that of grants to public and other bodies. Between 1962 and 1965, grants to government organizations grew from $6.9 million to $12.1 million and by 1966 reached approximately $14 million. Private grants went from $2.7 million in 1962 to $6.9 million in 1965 and an estimated $7.5 million in 1966. Grants to county councils increased from $8.9 million in 1962 to $14.5 million in 1965 and were estimated to be $15.5 million in 1966. Other examples of increased subventions appear in Table 9.4.

Grants were rising at a rate of about 20 percent per year, while revenue was growing at about 8 percent. The first step to control this trend was to place a ceiling on all grants at the 1965 level and place the onus of justification on those seeking the grant. The second step was to require government projects to move progressively toward balancing revenues with expenditure. To force the pace, the government eliminated the grants completely in favor of viable enterprises and loans. The result was greater scrutiny of operations without undesirable forms of control. In effect, the treasury assumed the position of a banker in its relations with these enterprises rather than its former position of guarantor.

The government deployed a number of other instruments to control public expenditure, such as the conversion of scholarship grants into loans repayable by a specified number of years of government service.

Table 9.4. Grants to Public and Other Bodies

Authority	1962	1965	1966
Marketing Board	$ 32,000	$200,000	$ 228,851
Board of Industrial Training	162,700	207,450	227,354
Carnegie Free Library	103,164	133,152	124,264
Queen's Hall Board	26,785	65,528	43,823
Lady Hochoy Home for Retarded Children	67,790	106,730	123,500
International Development Corporation	525,000	999,285	997,471
Tourist Board	445,285	689,495	1,085,805

Source: *Hansard Reports*, 6 (1965-1966):497-498.

This measure sought both to emphasize to holders of scholarships their obligations to their country and to reduce defaulting on scholarship loans. A United Nations consultant on in-service training and a central training unit in the Ministry of Finance assisted other departments in developing their own training schemes. New financial regulations were drafted, and a separate division under the minister of finance was established for financial accounting and administration.[2]

2. The latter was the recommendation of the commission of inquiry, which had been appointed to inquire into the accounts of the central government for the year 1961.

THE STATE OF THE ECONOMY

The basic reality in 1963 was an unforeseen deceleration in the growth rate of the entire economy. Between 1951 and 1962 the gross domestic product (GDP) at factor cost increased from $312.1 million to $1,005.7 million, while national income increased from $260.6 million to $779.0 million. Per capita, GDP thus grew from $481 in 1951 to $1,180 in 1962, which placed Trinidad and Tobago sixth in the western hemisphere in this area.[1] In terms of 1960 prices, between 1951 and 1961 real output increased by 8.5 percent per year and real national income by 6.6 percent per year, one of the highest growth rates in the world during that period. Between 1955 and 1961, the rate of growth was even higher, with the GDP increasing at a rate of 10 percent per year.

During the period 1951 to 1961 petroleum moved into first position in contribution to gross domestic product, from 29 percent of real output in 1951 to 32 percent in 1961. At the same time, the contribution of agriculture declined from 17.2 percent of real output in 1951 to 12 percent in 1961, while manufacturing and construction grew from 13 percent of real output to 16 percent, and the public sector declined from 14 percent to 12 percent of output. Together, however, agriculture, petroleum, sugar refining, manufacturing, and construction remained at about the same level, or just under 62 percent of output.[2] The performance of the petroleum sector resulted from expansion both in the production of crude oil and in refining.

The comparison in Table 10.1 illustrates the relative growth rates in various sectors of the economy. The comparatively poor performance of agriculture is striking; changes in the relative contributions of the various components to the overall sector during the period are even more revealing. The contribution of sugar rose from 21.4 percent to 27.4 percent; that of tree crops (cocoa, citrus, coffee, and copra) declined from 27.7 percent to 21.9 percent. Domestic agriculture, representing principally food production (ground provisions, vegetables, and fruit), declined from 34.2 percent to 26.6 percent. Livestock and fish-

1. The leading five were the United States, Canada, Venezuela, Puerto Rico, and Argentina.
2. *Second Five-Year Development Plan, 1964-1968* (Trinidad and Tobago: Government Printery, 1963), chap. 3.

APPRAISAL OF REFORMS **10**

Table 10.1. Growth Rates of Various Economic Sectors, 1951-1961

Sector	Growth Rate (%) 1951-1961
Petroleum	9.7
Agriculture	4.2
Manufacturing	9.7
Construction	6.6
Services (including tourism)	9.9
Transportation	8.5

ing, however, almost solely as a result of a spectacular increase in poultry production, rose from 13.2 percent of agriculture in 1957 to 21.8 percent in 1961. The failure of agriculture was all the more serious for having occurred in a period of strong domestic demand.

The newest sector, manufacturing, responded well to liberal incentives embodied primarily in the aid-to-pioneer-industries legislation, while construction reacted favorably to the stimulus of the government's five-year development program beginning in 1958 and the expansion in the petroleum industry. The services sector failed to expand facilities in transportation, distribution and commerce, and banking and finance. Expenditures by visitors and tourists (included in the service sector) rose from $6 million in 1951 to $14.8 million in 1961.

Comparable changes took place in demand. Private consumption increased in real terms by 7.5 percent per year between 1951 and 1961, government consumption expenditure by 5.1 percent, and capital formation by 9.8 percent. Fixed capital formation increased by 11.3 percent per year, exports of goods and services by 10.1 percent, and imports of goods and services by 9.6 percent.[3]

On the whole, investment, exports, and imports showed an increasing share of gross domestic expenditure (GDE) over the period, but the increase was largely in petroleum. Per capita consumption in real terms increased by 4.6 percent, while per capita national income in real terms increased by 3.5 percent, indicating a decline in the ratio of personal saving to personal income. Indications for the future show up vividly in

3. *Ibid.*

the rapid increase in expenditure on consumer durables and foreign travel, in contrast to the low level of expenditure on, for example, home maintenance. The overall picture shows a decline in the proportion of gross national savings (GNS) to GDP, with an average of 14 percent in 1951, falling to an average of 13 percent over the period of the first five-year development plan, 1958 to 1962.

According to the authors of the third five-year plan, "The period 1955 to 1961 displayed all the symptoms usually associated with an economic boom."[4] However, the real boom had come, according to the authors of the second five-year plan, in the second half of the decade. Petroleum exports led the way, with support from other sectors, mainly manufacturing and government, but with no help from agriculture. Wages increased rapidly during the period.[5] According to the authors of the second five-year development plan, "The oil boom of the late fifties was quite exceptional in that rising prices between 1956 and 1958 reinforced the phenomenal rate of expansion of both crude and petroleum products between 1956 and 1961."[6]

Independence literally came at the end of a boom, and there had been no warning that the end was coming. The end of the boom is reflected in the statistics relating to finance. Table 10.2 illuminates conditions in central government finance.

Thus, before the end of the first five-year plan and immediately prior to independence, three developments of considerable significance were in progress: (1) a dramatic decline in the current account surplus and a consequent decline in the contribution to development from this source; (2) the exhaustion of surplus balances; and (3) expenditure rising at a considerably faster rate than revenue.

Of perhaps even greater significance was that all these developments took place during the period of boom and immediately before the deceleration in the rate of growth in 1963. Throughout the period following independence, the results of these developments continued to cause

4. *Draft Third Five-Year Plan, 1969-1973* (Trinidad and Tobago: Government Printery, 1968), p. 22.
5. The index of wage rates (February = 100) for nonagricultural workers in firms employing ten persons or more increased from 71.2 in February 1951 to 162.6 in May 1962. In government, the increase was from 72.6 in February 1951 to 179.2 in May 1962. The increase was sharper between 1956 and 1962 than between 1951 and 1956—9 percent per year as against 8 percent per year.
6. *Draft Second Five-Year Plan, 1964-1968*, p. 33.

Table 10.2 Central Government Finance, 1956-1961 (in millions of dollars)

	1956	1957	1958	1959	1960	1961
Total current receipts	87.9	101.1	129.8	133.2	148.7	145.5
Total current expenditure	62.1	67.5	79.0	89.4	100.8	118.7
Salaries	27.3	35.8	32.2	40.2	43.6	48.4
Interest	3.5	2.8	2.8	2.8	3.3	4.1
Supplies and service	31.3	28.9	44.0	46.4	53.9	66.2
Current surplus before transfers	25.8	33.6	50.8	43.8	47.9	26.8
Current transfers	12.7	14.0	16.6	15.8	18.1	21.5
Current surplus	13.1	19.6	34.2	28.0	29.8	5.3
Capital expenditure	25.5	22.2	37.0	29.5	37.4	61.7
Overall surplus (+) or deficit (–)	-10.4	-2.6	-2.8	-1.5	-7.5	-56.4

Source: *Financial Statistics, 1965-1966* (Trinidad and Tobago: Central Statistical Office, 1966), p. 2.

real headaches, and much effort was devoted to arresting and reversing the trends they indicated. Recognizing the gravity of the problem, the framers of the second five-year development plan emphasized:

The first point to be made is that on present indications recurrent revenues are hardly likely to make any direct contribution to the financing of development expenditure. However, such revenues are projected to make an indirect contribution through meeting additional public debt charges in respect of non-self-liquidating loans raised to finance the Programme and by covering increased recurrent expenditure resulting from the Programme.[7]

Against this projection, the actual performance can be seen in Table 10.3.

THE POLICY FRAMEWORK

The policy framework of the measures introduced was set out in budget speeches from 1962 to 1967 and in the Second Five-Year Development Plan, 1964-1968. Speaking on behalf of the government in reply to queries concerning the direction in which the country was likely to move during independence, the minister of finance described the economic system the administration intended to promote: "Our aim is a

7. *Second Five-Year Development Plan,* chap. 7 ("Size and Financing of Public Sector Outlays"), par. 26.

Table 10.3. Central Government Finance, 1962-1966 (in millions of dollars)

	1962	1963	1964	1965	1966
Total current receipts	166.7	185.4	202.9	206.2	214.3
Total current expenditure	128.7	137.7	150.8	157.8	161.1
Salaries	53.6	56.9	60.5	63.5	83.3
Interest	5.3	7.3	8.3	11.4	12.0
Supplies and services	69.8	73.5	82.0	82.9	65.8
Current surplus before transfers	38.0	47.7	52.1	48.4	53.2
Current transfers	25.4	31.2	38.7	35.3	42.5
Current surplus	12.6	16.5	13.4	13.1	10.7
Capital expenditure	57.8	59.6	75.1	57.6	62.9
Overall surplus (+) or deficit (-)	-45.2	-43.1	-61.7	-44.5	-52.2

Source: *Financial Statistics, 1967-1968* (Trinidad and Tobago: Central Statistical Office, 1968), Table 3, pp. 2-3.

free society in which Government and private enterprise work together in partnership to promote the country's development and to make available the fruits of industry to an ever-increasing number of our citizens."[8]

This was a clear commitment to a strong role for private enterprise in the society, though the definition of the relationship between the private sector and the government extended no further than the rather flexible use of the term "partnership." Nevertheless, the small size of the country was emphasized as a powerful constraint in exercising options. In the 1963 budget debate the minister of finance outlined the problem:

The smaller the domestic market, the more dependent a country becomes on overseas trade, and the more involved in international complications. This means simply that the alternatives available to a very small country are much more limited than those available to a very large country. I think we in Trinidad and Tobago must face the fact that we do not have much choice in the pattern of our industrial development.

Given the small size of our own domestic market and our consequent need for external markets, . . . efficiency and competitiveness are primary considerations in our industrial development. Thus, while on the one hand we have to recognize that it takes some time for the inexperi-

8. *Hansard Reports*, 1 (1961-1962):660.

enced local population to develop the necessary skills and outlook needed for successful industrialisation, we also have to recognise that the need to sell abroad makes it suicidal to attempt to carry for an indefinite period any burden of high cost, low efficiency, and uncompetitive local industries.[9]

On the question of the attitude toward foreign capital, the minister stated:

While the Government will therefore make every possible effort to increase employment in the short run by the most effective combination of labor with other factors of production, in the long run an appreciable increase in the number of permanent jobs will only be achieved by an appreciable expansion of the productive resources of the country.

This in turn demands funds for continued investment which, together with the widespread and legitimate demand for social improvement, it is impossible to finance entirely from our domestic savings. Honorable Members will therefore understand the framework within which the Government has offered and will continue to offer special incentives to investors principally in the fields of industry, hotel development, housing, and agriculture and will continue to extend to them a warm welcome so long as they are prepared to abide by the country's labor policies and its laws.[10]

On the general question of industrialization, the government adopted the conclusions on the subject of the United Nations World Economic Survey, 1961, in particular the conclusion that the ultimate objective of underdeveloped countries should be "to construct industrial economies as diversified as those which now exist in the advanced countries." The survey fully took into account the problems of unemployment, underemployment, and low productivity in developing countries and demonstrated the inadequacy of expansion based on external demand as the means to economic development.

For Trinidad and Tobago, one of the most urgent requirements was a review of the incentive legislation that had been passed in the early fifties and on occasion amended on a piecemeal basis. As of 1970, no such review had taken place.

In the industrialization process, preference was given as a matter of policy to import substitution and export production. In this context, the essence was savings—government, private, individual, corporate. Profits were a means to generate savings for reinvestment. In the 1965

9. *Ibid.*, vol. 1, part 1 (1962-1963), p. 878.
10. *Ibid.*, 1 (1961-1962):660.

budget speech, the minister of finance expressed the following view on profits:

Corporate savings or savings by business firms can only be sustained through profits of business enterprises whether private or government-owned. It makes no sense at all, consequently, whether in a free enterprise or in a socialist economy, to generate hostility against profits. Such hostility is self-defeating and destructive. What is of vital importance is the use to which profits are put, that is to say, whether profits are reinvested to add to capital formation and employment or whether they are merely distributed or dissipated in consumption.[11]

Government policy considered it inequitable to allow price increases to erode the workers' standard of living simply to improve profit margins. "If workers are going to be asked to show moderation in their wage demands," the minister of finance stated, "the businessmen must also be asked to show moderation in their pricing policies. Restraint in one direction must be matched by restraint in the other direction."[12]

This need for moderation and restraint, especially in the absence of legislative measures, was emphasized in the conclusion of the report of the International Labor Office on "Employment Objectives in Economic Development" of 1961, which particularly stresses the need for a high level of investment:

We believe that, provided effective restraints are at the same time imposed on the consumption of other, and especially more privileged, groups in society, and for as long as there continues to be much unemployment and underemployment, it is very very important that there should be moderation and restraint in demanding, and in conceding, wage increases in the modern sector. We believe that without such moderation and restraint it will be harder and perhaps impossible to provide productive work for those who desperately need it, for the following reasons:

(a) Wage rises in the modern sector may induce the adoption of labour-saving techniques and a shift of production toward goods requiring more capital and less labor to produce.

(b) Rising wages in the private sector will sooner or later induce imitative wage and salary increases in the public sector which will reduce the budgetary resources available for public capital formation and other developmental expenditure, including education and vocational training and for social services for the relief of those whose needs are greatest.

(c) Wage increases are accompanied by an increase in consumption which is mainly reserved for those who are already fully employed; this

11. *Ibid.*, 4 (1965):1052-1053.
12. *Ibid.*, p. 1053.

imposes demands on scarce resources required for investment and for additional consumption by the newly employed.

(d) High labour costs in the modern sector may prevent prices of industrial products from falling as much as would be warranted by the general advances in productivity. Thus, the cost of capital formation (and so of new jobs) is kept high, to the detriment of both public investment and agriculture, which need industrial goods from the modern sector for their development; this will tend to make for less food production (because of low investment in real terms), higher food prices, and a higher cost of living.

(e) High prices due to high wage costs may impair the competitive position of potential exporters.

(f) Finally, a widening gap in earning levels between the modern and the traditional sectors will tend to induce a growing number of people to search for jobs in the modern sector when such jobs are increasing at a relatively slow rate; this will swell official unemployment figures and put an extra burden on public budgets.[13]

Referring to the effects of massive wage increases on employment and the balance of payments, the minister of finance remarked in the 1965 budget speech:

I have already referred to the erroneous belief that increases in wages and salaries will lead to increased demand and consequently increased investment and employment. This belief, I have already pointed out, is unsound in theory and is contradicted by the facts of our recent economic history. The demand generated by such increases is in effect for goods and services produced outside of Trinidad and Tobago and the resulting increased employment is for workers outside of Trinidad and Tobago.[14]

What was under scrutiny here were the limitations of classic Keynesian analysis when applied to the specific circumstances of Trinidad and Tobago.

Finally, in proposing the extensive measures outlined in the 1963 budget, the minister of finance summarized these guiding considerations:

Revenues will be raised with three major considerations in mind:
Firstly, the economic necessities arising from our trading position.
Secondly, considerations of social justice.
Thirdly, the need for the Government to continue unswervingly in its development effort.[15]

13. International Labor Office, "Employment Objectives in Economic Development," (ILO Report of a meeting of experts, Geneva), 1961, pp. 56-57.
14. *Hansard Reports*, 4(1965):1051-1052.
15. *Ibid.*, vol. 1, part 1(1962-1963), p. 912.

FISCAL AND INSTITUTIONAL MEASURES

The third five-year development plan offers this summary of the degree of fiscal and institutional reforms attained:

The public sector spent some $306 million on capital expenditure. This represented some 95 percent of the Plan Target of $320 million. Performance in physical terms, while creditable, was not quite as good as the financial performance because of increase in costs and prices. Some 60 percent of actual expenditure was financed from internal resources, as compared with a planned target of 30 percent. Furthermore, as we shall see, the public sector was able to carry through most of the policies and institutional changes to which it had committed itself in the Plan. On the other hand, activity on the part of the local private sector in agriculture, manufacturing, fishing, tourism and house construction was much less than expected.[16]

Overall performance of the economy indicated a growth of approximately 4.5 percent of GDP or, if we allow for an annual population growth of just under 2 percent, a per capita growth rate just about equal to what the plan envisaged. Unemployment remained at the 1962 percentage level as the plan projected. Up to 1967, the cost of living was holding steady at an average annual rate of increase of just over 2 percent:[17]

September

1960	100.0
1961	101.1
1962	104.1
1963	108.1
1964	109.1
1965	110.9
1966	115.5
1967	117.9[18]

Perhaps the most striking fact is that domestic financing of the 1964-1968 five-year development plan exceeded the plan target by over 100 percent. Table 10.4 sets out the estimated and actual financing of the plan.

Successful financing of the plan was due largely to the excellent per-

16. *Draft Third Five-Year Plan, 1969-1973*, p. 51.
17. In 1968, devaluation of the Trinidad and Tobago dollar and indirect taxes imposed in the 1968 budget caused the retail price index to rise by over 12 points to 130.0.
18. *Draft Third Five-Year Plan, 1969-1973*, p. 49.

Table 10.4. Five-Year Development Plan, 1964-1968: Estimated and Actual Financing (in millions of dollars)

	Estimate	Revised Estimate	Actual
Public sector savings (including government revenue surplus and savings of public utilities)	41.6	45.4	67.2
Use of government surplus balances	—	—	—
Capital revenues from local sources	6.0	4.0	3.0
Local borrowing	47.6	65.5	116.0
Foreign borrowing	66.1	53.0	68.8
Chaguaramas agreement funds	50.5	51.5	51.0
Foreign aid (grants and soft loans)	90.8	101.1	—
	302.6[a]	320.5[b]	306.0[c]

[a]See *Draft Third Five-Year Plan, 1969-1973*, p. 49.
[b]*Draft Five-Year Plan, 1964-1968*, p. 93.
[c]*Second Five-Year Plan, 1964-1968*, Modifications to Draft Plan, p. 9.

formance in public sector savings and local borrowing. Though none of the $101 million foreign aid forecast was realized, foreign borrowing and funds under the Chaguaramas agreement were received in substantially the amounts anticipated.

The 50 percent increase in public sector savings over the estimate was largely the product of the fiscal and institutional reforms culminating in the Finance Act of 1966. Over the three-year period 1966-1968, receipts from withholding taxes alone amounted to approximately $12 million,[19] and receipts from corporation taxes totaled $166,450,000. A resurgence in oil production in 1967 further strengthened the treasury position.

Import duty receipts actually declined from $48 million in 1967 to $45.2 million in 1968 in spite of increased duties that year and the upward movement in import prices stemming from devaluation. The distribution of British Caribbean currency board assets upon dissolution in 1964 realized $9 million in 1967, and the Central Bank transferred to its reserve account and to the treasury $10.8 million during the period 1964-1968.

19. Over the same period total development expenditure in Tobago amounted to $12.17 million.

During the first six months of 1967, following passage of the insurance act, insurance companies purchased almost $8 million in government bonds, and by December 13, 1967, government securities in the statutory fund established by the act had increased to $13 million, an increase of $10 million from a year before.

An increase in private sector savings paralleled the increase in public sector savings. Private sector savings in commercial banks increased by about 63 percent over the period 1963-1968, while overall deposit liabilities increased by 61 percent, as shown in Table 10.5. Total liabilities of the commercial banks showed a steady increase. At the same time savings deposits and deposit liabilities increased.

Savings actually exceeded the capacity of the economy to absorb them. Lacking were the appropriate institutional forms to channel them fully into productive employment, and there was a lack of effective demand for funds from the private sector. Much of the additional savings was funneled into public sector expenditure on the development program.[20]

Table 10.5. Commercial Bank Liabilities and Deposits, 1962-1967 (in thousands of dollars)

Year	Commercial Bank Liabilities	Savings Deposits	Deposit Liabilities
1962	212,219	96,941	202,771
1963	252,999	106,959	240,533
1964	267,107	114,783	247,703
1965	286,157	121,047	267,667
1966	300,538	128,645	273,186
1967	311,502	140,977	293,106

Source: *Annual Statistical Digest* (Trinidad and Tobago: Central Statistical Office, 1967), pp. 146, 147, 149.

20. The Trinidad and Tobago Federation of Chambers of Industry and Commerce, Inc., while generally critical of the government's fiscal policies for "depriving the private sector of much needed funds," itself replied to criticism in the 1969-1973 plan that addressed itself to the lending policies of the commercial banks: "The wording of paragraph 85 suggests that the productive sector was starved of finance by the commercial banks at the expense of financing consumer credit. This is unjust, as in the first place, *we know of no viable productive enterprise which was unable to raise commercial bank finance.*" See *Draft Third Five-Year Development Plan, 1969-1973, Trinidad and Tobago, Preliminary Comments*

Taking into account the performance in the public sector and the availability of savings in the private sector, we can see that the 1969-1973 development plan shed light upon the causes of the latter's sluggishness:

What appeared to be more evident was the tendency to highlight and indeed exaggerate the inhibiting effects of the negative instruments and a reluctance to take advantage of the positive instruments. Policies were judged in terms of highly abstract models of the workings of an ideal and probably historically non-existent type of free enterprise economy, without sufficient reference to the concrete problem of needs and possibilities of the Trinidad and Tobago economy. In addition, not enough attention was paid to the need in many cases for upgrading the levels of expertise in private firms—particularly with respect to management and supervision, industrial relations, accounting and marketing, especially export marketing.[21]

The defensive reaction of the private sector throughout the period of the reforms and the period of the development plan was summed up in the same document:

In the first eighteen months of the plan, the unsettled state of labour relations was adduced by way of explanation of the lack of vigour in this sector. With the passing of the 1965 Industrial Act, attention then shifted to the deterioration of the investment climate alleged to be a consequence of the Finance Act of 1966. The amendments to the Finance Act introduced in the 1968 Budget on the recommendation of the Tripartite Fiscal Review Committee were not in 1968 followed by any resurgence of activity: the blame was shifted to the impact on consumer spending of the 1968 sharp increases in indirect taxation and to the delays in securing physical planning and other types of investment approval.[22]

More basic weaknesses undoubtedly lay in the traditional orientation of the business sector toward commerce, the inhibiting corporate structure based on the private company, the reliance on foreign capital and expertise, and the lack of opportunities for formal training in business methods and administration, as well as distrust of the new orientation and base of political power. In short, the private sector had yet to come

---

(Trinidad and Tobago: Chamber of Industry and Commerce, March 31, 1969), p. 25. Earlier in the document, the chamber declared, "Taxes were increased across a narrow, direct tax base. This unwittingly struck at the heart of the development mechanism and, at a time of stagnation in the economy, contributed to a scarcity of local investment funds . . ." (ibid., p. 6).
21. *Draft Third Five-Year Plan, 1969-1973*, p. 98.
22. *Ibid.*

to terms with the nationalist movement and its objective of economic and social transformation, and the major weakness of the development plan was its reliance on the private sector during the plan period to achieve too much of its own transformation.

Dynamics of Transformation 3

THE MOTIVE POWER OF NATIONALISM

It is of the utmost importance, in considering the significance of nationalism, to appreciate that not a single community on earth has been able to maintain its identity or freedom in the absence of organization as a nation-state. Toynbee points out that the application of the institution of nation-state has produced great mischief in countries in which it has been an artificially introduced innovation rather than a spontaneous native growth. K. A. Busia, the African sociologist, has underlined the point by drawing attention to the geographical boundaries in Africa, drawn by the colonial powers, which often separated not only ethnic and linguistic groups but even families.[1] Yet these boundaries, with modifications, are the frontiers of the new nation-states.

Nationalism and technology gave Europeans an irresistible power in other lands. European empires grew while other peoples and civilizations were subjugated or obliterated. The highly advanced Incas and Aztecs were no more fortunate than primitive societies such as the Caribs and Arawaks. The Ethiopians, Persians, and Chinese all succumbed to the new dynamic European civilization, which was highly organized and tooled.

Conquest inspired feelings of superiority, theories of active and passive peoples, of higher and lower nations, races, even continents. Tennyson was offering more than a poetic fancy when in "Locksley Hall" he declared, "Better fifty years of Europe than a cycle [age] of Cathay." Twentieth-century nationalism was simply a natural reaction to eighteenth- and nineteenth-century nationalism that had turned into imperialism. Nehru illustrated the point in his autobiography:

The initial urge came to me, I suppose, through pride both individual and national, and the desire, common to all men, to resist another's domination and have freedom to live the life of our choice. It seemed monstrous to me that a great country like India, with a rich and immemorial past, should be bound hand and foot to a far-away island which imposed its will upon her. . . . The whole ideology of British rule was that of the master race, and the structure of government was based upon it. . . . I would have preferred any kind of resistance to this whatever the consequences, rather than that our people should endure this treatment.[2]

1. K. A. Busia, *The Challenge of Africa* (New York: Praeger, 1962).
2. Jawaharlal Nehru, *The Discovery of India* (London: Meridian, 1951), p. 304.

African nationalism makes the identical demand. "Africans," says Busia, "demand acceptance as equals in the human family."[3]

However, just as nationalism is a liberating force, it can also be a restricting one. While throwing off empires, it often crystallizes internal divisions. The tragedy of modern Africa is a proliferation of nation-states that has created irrational weaknesses and barriers exploited by the most entrenched enemies of African self-determination. The Caribbean area, with its extreme fragmentation, offers an even more graphic example of the absurdities of misdirected sentiments of nationalism.

THE CASE OF TRINIDAD AND TOBAGO

The theme of reform during the three or four decades before independence was limited almost exclusively to the political arena, the desire of the local population being first to influence those in power, then to share the power, and finally to wield it alone. This conformed to the general pattern of political development within the British Empire, though Trinidad and Tobago was hardly in the vanguard of the general advance.

The Second World War produced a dramatic acceleration in the movement toward self-determination that inevitably reached Trinidad and Tobago, not to mention other, even smaller Caribbean communities. It is a tribute to the good sense of the population that there was a large measure of agreement that an effective federation of the Caribbean ought to be a major goal of nation building. The establishment of such a federation, however, proved beyond the capacities of West Indian leadership. The most significant achievement of the PNM was the orderly transfer of political power amid the chaotic conditions ensuing from the breakdown of the federation.

With independence, political reform came to an end, though many would have preferred to go a step further toward becoming a republic like India or Ghana rather than to continue in the close application of the Westminster model of a constitutional monarchy. Social and economic reconstruction then emerged as the major issue, later broadening to include the more sweeping question of the distribution and use of power within the national community. The issue became critical in the

3. Busia. *Challenge of Africa*, p. 139.

face of the government's apparent weaknesses in responding to pressures from business interests, a continuing high level of unemployment, and growing inequities in the methods of promoting industrial development. The condition led to public arguments as to the relative merits of the free-enterprise and socialist-oriented systems.[4]

Trinidad and Tobago has never possessed a free-enterprise system except in the most limited sense. The major decisions on production and distribution have always been either determined or at least decisively influenced by the state. Matters of capital, manpower, trading relationships, and financial and monetary arrangements have all been state determined since the time of Spanish colonialism.

J. R. Hicks, in his case study of development in Ceylon, asserts that a country is underdeveloped because it has not yet been profitable to develop.[5] However, it was the Spanish governor de Berrio's refusal to suppress the flourishing illicit trade in tobacco with the English and Dutch that brought him a reprimand. In colonial economics the touchstone of desirable development is not profitability itself but profitability to the metropolitan country.

A grasp of this ubiquitous feature of colonial economics is essential in order to understand both the structure of a colonial economy and the consequent necessity that state power in independence must bring about a structural transformation compatible with the quite different demands of an independent state.

The most fundamental question relating to the use of political power in an ex-colonial country is whether it can achieve in the economic field what was achieved under the imperial umbrella, namely, development along lines predetermined by the political authority to accord with the interests it represents. It goes without saying that the democratic base of political power in a country such as Trinidad and Tobago necessarily gives rise to representation of much broader interests than those that prevailed under the colonial administration.

The kind of political power contemplated here is inextricably bound to human dignity, human rights, and human freedoms. And apart from

4. See debate in the *Express* between James Millette, Thomas Gatcliffe, and Ken Gordon from Sunday, March 24, to Tuesday, April 30, 1968.
5. J. R. Hicks, *Essays in World Economics* (Oxford: Clarendon Press, 1959), p. 109.

these essential human considerations, such a political philosphy is, as R. K. Woetzel points out, "the best answer to the aggressive ideologies of our times."[6] all the more pertinent to a Caribbean area that has produced Trujillo, Batista, and Duvalier.

How to ensure that government does not become government of the many by the few in the interest of the few; how to counterbalance the corrupting influence of power; how to guarantee that the vast machinery of the state does not destroy the liberty and suppress the personality of the individual; how to ensure that men can disagree and honor another's right to disagree—all these are questions of great current concern in all the ex-colonial countries of the Caribbean.

All democratic regimes are committed to finding answers to these questions while they are finding solutions to economic problems, and since political power is the engine of economic reform, it seems useful to examine the foundation and exercise of that power in an ex-colonial democratic society committed to peaceful transformation of its economic and social structure.

First, however, some of the constraints and hazards to that transformation will be set forth in the next chapter.

6. R. K. Woetzel, *The Philosophy of Freedom* (Dobbs Ferry, N.Y.: Oceana, 1966), p. 45.

INTERNAL CONSTRAINTS

Ultimately the internal constraints on transformation are political. The most soundly conceived program cannot be carried out unless it has a solid foundation of political will and competence.

The major consideration here is the working of the political system. All developing countries have difficulties with their political systems. Most of those that were formerly part of the British Empire have adopted the Westminster model. Some, like Trinidad and Tobago and Jamaica, maintain the old form of a constitutional monarchy; or others, like India and Nigeria, have become republics with varying features of the presidential system.

Weaknesses in Developing Countries

A significant weakness in most developing countries is the absence of traditions in the use of political power within the democratic framework; hence, there are no precedents to follow. If precedents do exist, they are often insufficiently established or conductive to expedient departures. British precedents may or may not be followed but can always be rejected on the ground that circumstances in the United Kingdom are different. The tendency is to argue that whatever the leadership does is by definition the right thing.

Another weakness is the absence of a fully developed educational system and its professional organizations that operate independently of the government. Often universities are in their infancy and are dependent on state patronage. Professional bodies usually place high priority on having good relations with a strong government to ensure the welfare and advancement of their members. Business organizations concentrate almost exclusively on defending and promoting commercial interests, when they feel these interests are in even remote jeopardy, their criticism tends to be indiscriminately vituperative and sophistic. If they regard their interests as secure, their principal concern is for political stability at very nearly any cost to liberty or development. In some countries trade unions are the most independent and progressive groups in outlook; but in others they act merely as arms of the ruling political party.

Another deficiency is often the electorate's lack of experience in self-government. Followers tend to identify policies with personalities and often stick with them even after the policies have radically changed. In these circumstances, the responsibility of the leadership is immense, power is extensive, and the temptation to misuse it is great.

The Politics of Power

One of the few universal prerequisites to a genuine sense of nationhood is a leader who, through plain, subtle, or mysterious qualities, is able to demand and get from his people action and convictions that those before him have been either unwilling or unable to exact. Every nation has—or will have—one man it looks to as the symbol of nationhood itself.

Yet the qualities of leadership required to attain independence are wholly unlike those required to succeed in independence; and if transformation is to be achieved, the issue becomes not only the quality of the leadership potential but also its selection process. The man who leads his country to independence comes to prominence under quite different circumstances from those of the leaders who follow him. The national struggle has been waged for the single goal of independence, and when it is achieved, the atmosphere is euphoric. The major battle has been fought with the cohesive themes of unity, nationhood, equality.[1]

Auguries for the regime are usually favorable. The population has developed a sense of cohesion and purpose in the struggle for national liberation. The leader has become identified with the right policies. He represents and articulates the grievances, the yearnings, the desires for self-expression and recognition. The personality of the first leader after independence often attains a messianic character that successors, however deserving, cannot rival. And herein lies a danger.

In countries that achieve nationhood largely through the efforts of a political party, the leader of the party will also be the leader of the government. The government has, at least initially, enormous powers under the constitution, and the party leader is in a position of vast influence, in relation to both the party and the government. As political strategy develops, government as well as party powers are used against party dissidents. The ascendancy of government over party or of party

1. See Kwame Nkrumah, *I Speak of Freedom* (London: Heinemann, 1961, p. 106. See also Tom Mboya, *Freedom and After* (London: André Deutsch, 1963), p. 62, and the excellent novel by the Nobel Prize winner Miguel Angel Asturias, *The President* (London: Gollancz, 1963).

over government is a matter of the strength and position of personalities as well as organizations. The net effect in either case will be increased dependence on the leader.

Because lobbyists of all kinds prefer situations in which they can deal with a powerful individual upon whom they can use personal influence rather than situations in which they must deal with several or many individuals, powerful forces outside the party and constitutional framework are always at work to centralize the government and ensure a highly centralized leadership in the party; and the astute party leader is fully aware of the good will he can generate with favorable decisions toward vested interests. There is also concern for political stability, and it is always of considerable assistance to the strategy if there is a highly vocal band of avowed Communists who can be maneuvered into the position that the imperial power occupied before independence, as a foreign presence creating or aggravating internal ills.

In business circles, socialism is often equated with communism, and the tendency will be to identify anyone having slightly leftist views as having communistic inclinations. The climate and the system will have begun to eliminate all but party hacks from positions of power. The survivors will tend to be tough people skilled in political intrigue, highly ambitious, but hardly dedicated to the transformation of the society.

In these circumstances a great deal will depend on the leader's understanding of what is happening around him and his will to arrest it. He will find it at least difficult, perhaps impossible. What, in fact, will have been taking place is the erosion of his entire strategy of transformation.

Part of the difficulty is that aside from the independence movement attracting people committed to its objectives, the leader has built up a personal following including both admirers and persons who, not unnaturally, are fired by the expectation of reward for helping the leader gain power. Their loyalty is to the leader, and not to the movement; their attachment is more or less irrational, though often calculating; and their perspective is distorted. Among them are nearly equal portions of the idealistic and the opportunistic.

In the course of the struggle, some betray or defect. Their conduct does not set in motion the course of events, but it reinforces a trend. With the growth of the authority and stature of the leader, dissent becomes progressively less tolerated, and it is equated with disloyalty.

The first road to success is adulation of the leader, and one must know how to read the road signs.

The leader is in an extremely difficult position. He must be a shrewd enough judge of human nature to distinguish the false from the genuine. Moreover, because of the large numbers involved, he will not always have an opportunity to judge for himself. People become merely names, fleeting acquaintances, or correspondents. The leader must act through his agents and representatives, as it is impossible for him to deal with everyone himself. Through whom should he act: those who make him aware of his weaknesses or those who reinforce his strength; those who have doubts or those who are absolutely sure?

The war against idealism begins, at first low-keyed, tentative, and subtle. The situation becomes even more trying with a fractious opposition. The language of political debate between government and opposition grows harsh. Where the opposition cannot find criticisms, it invents them. Often it consists of elements that opposed the independence movement and starts with the disadvantage of being the antinationalist party and the party of reaction, attracting all the elements hostile to reform. The state of the opposition often illumines the state of the country. Another road to success is, therefore, to attack the opposition ostentatiously and in the presence of the leader.

Meanwhile, the leader's tactics will vary with the situation. If, for example, there are too many dissenting voices in the cabinet, he will gravitate toward the party and permit it a greater voice in running the government. If there is less trouble with the cabinet, he will gravitate toward the cabinet and keep the party from interferring in the government.

The case is similar in the various organs of the party. Consciously or unconsciously, the leader burdened with the cares of office looks for the path of least resistance. As head of government and as leader of the nation, he carries immense prestige, power, and patronage in his person. Organs or committees that demonstrate a life of their own can be frustrated or bypassed, or rival groups may be created.[2] When initiative and

2. Compare the tactics of Fidel Castro as outlined in Andrés Suárez's *Cuba: Castroism and Communism, 1959-1966* (Cambridge, Mass.: M.I.T. Press, 1967).

creativity are by these means thwarted, even though it is not the intention of the leader, a new situation emerges: everything becomes dependent on the leader.

At this stage the myth is propagated that everything the leader is associated with succeeds, and nothing will succeed without his blessing. Because the leader himself wishes some things to succeed and others to fail, he finds that such a pattern of thinking suits his own strategy.

Meanwhile, the government has been in office for some time, and the leader, being human, is bound to have made mistakes. The greater and more obvious the errors, the more shattering they can be to his authority and his prestige. The situation will not be improved by an admission of error, and so another factor of success comes into operation: a scapegoat must now be found to blame for every error.

The leader comes more and more to sense his power, and powerful personalities tend to disappear in the process. Weak ones rise in their place, and the word soon gets around that the leader makes or breaks. The leader is now supreme. But the country's economic and social problems are still to be resolved.

There may be spectacular successes. Little enough was attempted under the previous colonial administration. However, expectations in independence usually remain high, and problems are often complicated. Consequently the leadership recognizes the need for competence at the technical level. But competence at the technical level cannot offset weakness at the political level, and the technical cadres in the administrative service begin to feel frustrated. They follow the techniques that have been so successful at the top. They become aware of their power and begin to use it, and numerous opportunities appear: the award of contracts and of jobs, the issue and approval of plans and licenses, compensation for injuries. These are the means by which they can reward friends, punish enemies, and reap profits for the risks they take. The next stage is disillusionment and public discovery.

If the leader senses the dry rot early enough, his earlier qualities may reawaken and inspire him to arrest the deterioration. Or the deterioration will spread, eventually engulfing the populace and the institutions; it becomes part of the country. Then the leader and the country have failed to achieve true independence.

International Economics

In the struggle against the colonialism of the West, leaders of liberation movements have invariably adopted the ideas of the West. They instinctively find themselves on the side of Western champions of liberty. Tagore, Gandhi, Bandaranaike, Jinnah, U Nu, Nkrumah, Nyerere, and Kenyatta came to consider Jefferson, Thoreau, Rousseau, de Tocqueville, Locke, and Mill as much a part of their heritage as their own ancient civilizations. Yet it is these very nations, so justly proud of their revolutionary past, that today have become more interested in order than in equality, development, or liberty. No one understood this better than the late John F. Kennedy, who complained:

If the title deeds of history applied, it is we the American people who should be marching at the head of this worldwide revolution, counselling it, helping it to come to a healthy fruition. For whenever a local patriot emerges in Asia, the Middle East, Africa or Latin America to give form and focus to the forces of ferment he most often uses the great watchwords we once proclaimed to the world; equality of all souls, . . . the dignity of labor, . . . economic development broadly shared. . . . We have been made to appear as the defenders of the status quo, while the communists have portrayed themselves as the vanguard force pointing the way to a better, brighter and braver order of life.[3]

The fact is that the conservatism of the United States is not so much political as it is economic. American concern has come to be not so much with liberty as with economic interests. This sort of emphasis is the most powerful constraint on the movement for economic change, for it is the responsibility of industrialized countries to assist the less developed.

The power of foreign corporations in ex-colonial countries does not really lie in their own resources either within or outside the colonial economy. It lies rather in their ability to mobilize the resources of other corporations and ultimately those of foreign governments, the most powerful of which is the United States. In the face of such awesome power, many reformist leaders have given in to what appeared to them as unalterable reality. But the issue of control by foreign corporations demands reform, not resignation. Above all, technicians and political

3. John F. Kennedy, *Strategy of Peace* (New York: Harper, 1960), p. 6.

leaders in the United States must be made to understand the full, long-range consequences of its policies in the new countries.

A policy framework that imposes external political constraints over and above the constraints of the Universal Declaration of Human Rights places the less developed country in a position of subordination and is to that extent neocolonialist. Such policies are all the more debilitating when added to the already onerous internal constraints at work against a leadership struggling to bring about economic transformation.

The first basic question the leadership encounters is whether the discipline required for economic transformation is compatible with freedom. How much compulsion is proper within the basic framework of freedom? Here the choice is not between state ownership and individual ownership or between public and private enterprise. The choices are between centralization and decentralization, imposition and participation, voluntary compliance and compulsion. However, the difficulties do not end simply by choosing the methods for disposing of them.

It was shown earlier that a comprehensive program of reforms can be processed within a very short time. Two factors rendering the program more difficult to carry into effect were public pressure for immediate benefits and the complete lack of previous long-range planning and preparation. The result was a very limited understanding among the population of what its government was attempting to do, with inadequate means of tempering the explosive character of the demands.

In fact, a very special feature of the period of the reforms in Trinidad and Tobago was the unexpected deceleration in growth and national earnings occurring simultaneously with a sharp decrease in national expectations, factors usually discounted by institutions such as the International Monetary Fund. Officials of the IMF have not indicated that they consider the achievement of independence of the slightest significance. They also show little awareness of the implications of economic transformation, largely because of the history, structure, and aims of the fund, designed to meet the needs of developed countries.

Upon attaining independence, how should the nation finance its defense and its external representation? What should be the position of a country that recognizes these demands but is also, and for the first time, free to institute savings, investment, and social programs? It is obvious that the same assumptions that underlie the approach to fiscal and monetary matters in countries that have long enjoyed freedom cannot possibly be effective in newly independent countries. Yet very often officials of the IMF give the impression that this is precisely what they do assume.

International financial institutions such as the World Bank and the IMF recognize only in theory the need for economic transformation; their actual policies and views militate against it. An obvious example is their insistence on international tendering for the performance of contracts, which immediately places the highly organized and technically equipped firms of the developed countries in a position of advantage to carry out development projects in the less developed countries. There are also many subtler ways in which external considerations or private interests may override the national interests of a country in transformation.

It is the existence of these external constraints that constitutes the best justification for external aid and negotiated adjustments in trading arrangements, apart from the intrinsic inequities in the trading relationships themselves. External aid is a matter neither of charity nor of self-interest in the narrow sense; it is purely and simply a means of softening the harsh features of the system itself, a means of redirecting to the less fortunate countries resources that have accrued to the wealthier countries through the inequities of the international economic system, the natural working of which tends to accentuate the disparities in wealth rather than to reduce them.

This problem will probably become very acute during the next twenty-five years, as developing countries intensify their efforts toward economic transformation. External aid and adjusted trading arrangements will have to play an essential role in the international economic system if that system is to survive.

The Brain Drain

The continuing loss of skilled personnel has come to be one of the most crucial problems in less developed countries. It is a highly complex phenomenon that until lately was the subject of far less attention than the attraction or loss of capital, though there has been a recently quickening realization that human resources, especially skilled resources, are at least as important to economic transformation as the classic factors of production—land, labor, capital, and entrepreneurship.

The problem, of course, is not confined to less developed countries. Over the five-year period 1956-1961, 48 percent of Canada's graduating engineers emigrated to the United States. Norway annually loses an estimated 25 percent of her graduating engineers; Switzerland, 22.4 percent; the Netherlands, 21.8 percent; Greece, 20.7 percent. And the loss of scientists to the United States has become a matter of deep public concern in the United Kingdom.

The chief recipient of the brain drain is, of course, the United States, which in 1967 alone attracted over 10,000 professional immigrants from less developed countries, some 15 percent of them natural scientists.[4] There is a flow of technicians from developed to less developed countries, but the proportionate advantage is clearly to the former. In 1967, for example, the United States provided technical assistance to the extent of 1,500 technicians to eleven particular nations, but in the same year it took in from the same eleven nations 5,189 scientists, engineers, and physicians. In that year the United Kingdom lost 3,000 professional people to overseas positions, but at the same time was attracting 5,000 foreign professionals. Moreover, technicians on overseas missions from developed countries are usually on short-term assignments and cannot really be considered losses.

Few countries maintain comprehensive statistics relating to the movement of skilled personnel. The problem in Trinidad and Tobago can be at least inferred, however, from statistics on the movement of the personnel in the country's health services. From 1963 to 1968, 667 nurses graduated, but in the same year 432 resigned; from 1965 to 1968, 75 doctors joined the health services, but 46 resigned. Over the period 1963-1968, 10 dentists began practice, and 13 emigrated. During the same period, many other skilled employees were lost—engineering maintenance workers, orthopedic technicians, laboratory technicians, scientific assistants, radiologists, and radiographers, to name a few.[5] Table 12.1 illustrates the movement of doctors in the public service. The movement of nurses into and out of the public service tells an even more dramatic tale (see Table 12.2). The statistics disclose not only

4. United Nations, Secretariat, *Outflow of Trained Personnel from Developing Countries,* November 5, 1968.
5. Paper presented by the Trinidad and Tobago delegation to the Caribbean Health Ministers' Conference, 1969.

Table 12.1. Movement of Doctors in the Public Service

Year	Doctors Recruited	Doctors Resigned
1966	19	9
1967	33	17
1968	23	20
Total	75	46

Source: Paper presented by the Trinidad and Tobago delegation to the Caribbean Health Ministers' Conference.

Table 12.2. Movement of Nurses in the Public Service

Year	Students Recruited	Persons Qualifying	Resignation of Qualified Nurses
1964	154	125	36
1965	195	127	58
1966	175	131	73
1967	112	184	112
1968	211	100	153
Total	847	667	432

Source: Paper presented by the Trinidad and Tobago delegation to the Caribbean Health Ministers' Conference.

Table 12.3. Resignations among Experienced Nursing Personnel

Year	Under 1 Year	1 Year	2 Years	3 Years	4 Years	5 or More Years
1962	2	18	5	7	3	5
1963	4	10	16	7	5	4
1964	2	7	9	4	1	10
1965	3	4	11	16	11	12
1966	4	6	9	13	16	25
11 months of 1967	1	11	15	11	13	48

Source: Paper presented by the Trinidad and Tobago delegation to the Caribbean Health Ministers' Conference.

that the number of resignations is rising but that the rise is out of proportion to the numbers of those qualifying as nurses. The figures in Table 12.3 show also a rising proportion of resignations among experienced nursing personnel. But the problem extends to other professionals, such as teachers and engineers and skilled craftsmen such as mechanics.[6]

No single factor is by itself responsible for the outflow of skilled personnel. No doubt, if financial rewards were sufficiently high, people would be willing to undergo conditions that they would not otherwise tolerate: they would accept the extra payment as sufficient compensation for hardship. Conversely, they might stay home, even with inadequate financial rewards, if they could be made aware that the risks, expense, and other disadvantages of going to live abroad are often found to be insufficiently compensated by financial gain and reportedly better opportunities for advancement..

Other things being equal, the extent of the reward differential will be the major deciding factor. But in matters of living conditions or career environment, things are never equal. People whose capital is skill or art do not behave the same way toward reward differentials as people whose capital is money do toward attractive interest rates. This is simply because the former cannot relocate their capital without also relocating themselves. The decision to emigrate will be a product of a series of pluses and minuses. Weighing against migration will be the extensive array of personal, professional, cultural, and national attachments.

The state can hardly regulate such attachments, so attention in less developed countries should focus on improving career opportunities, job satisfaction, and financial rewards. Appeals to nationalist sentiments will seldom prove effective because the economic policies of most of these countries generally revolve around incentives rather than compulsion. The skilled person may find himself in a very real state of conflict as to whether his decisions should be those of a citizen responding to nationalistic appeals or those of a controller of capital responding to interest rates. The system of incentives thus makes nonsense of nationalistic appeals; its keystone is the attraction of foreign capital.

6. *Third Five-Year Development Plan, 1969-1973* (Trinidad and Tobago: Government Printery, 1968), chap. 12 ("Human Resources and Manpower Planning").

The difficult question that arises is: Why should investment in hotels, cosmetics, automobile assembly plants, zippers, and handbags receive high rewards, while investment in science, arts, engineering, and medicine receive low rewards? The answer to this question will scarcely be made on the grounds of nationalism. In such circumstances, appeals to nationalism may exercise some influence at the recruitment stage, but the effect is likely to diminish with experience.

As financial rewards are lower in the less developed country, the decisive factors in favor of keeping its skilled people from emigrating are likely to be career opportunity and job satisfaction, and the latter is likely to be the more crucial factor. It involves such matters as attitudes of supervisors toward subordinates, grievance procedures, and fair employment practices. It is here that the general political and social climate will come into play, as it will inevitably be reflected in conditions of employment.

An anti-intellectual political and social climate cannot attract intellectuals; one that produces a high turnover in the trained and skilled people is unlikely to attract such people; one that discourages dissent is unlikely to produce a critical faculty or initiative. A pronounced brain drain is only the symptom of more basic deficiencies in the whole society. The number of people who emigrate may be only a measure of those who have the opportunity to do so and thus may be only a small proportion of those who would like to leave.

Physical restraint is an inhuman way of solving the brain drain. Indeed, it often has the reverse effect. Contractual arrangements, on the other hand, are legitimate and even desirable. The state may legitimately require those who receive their education at public expense to defray its cost either by straight repayment or through service in their fields for a specified length of time upon completion of their studies.

Restrictions on immigration that highly developed countries might impose on personnel from less developed countries are not likely to solve the problem of the brain drain and could easily aggravate racial problems. Realism demands the appreciation that a certain level of drain is a quite predictable consequence of a system that in so many ways favors the rich over the poor, the developed over the less developed. It is part of the whole inexorable process of "cumulative causation," which Gunnar Myrdal has so admirably described in its application to the countries of Southeast Asia[7] and which cannot be finally corrected without the massive redistribution of resources that so worries the nations responsible for the problem.

7. Gunnar Myrdal, *Asian Drama* (New York: Twentieth Century Fund, 1968).

The aim of the politics of power is to imbue the people with confidence in their leader; the aim of the politics of transformation is to assist the people in building confidence in themselves. Political development must not end with the attainment of independence; independence is a culmination only of the movement toward self-government. The colonial regime instilled in the population its dependence upon the resources and administrative capabilities of the imperial power. A spirit of dependence, however, whether on the leader or on an imperial power, is incompatible with self-reliance, and that spirit is the first requisite in a successful struggle toward economic transformation.

K. A. Busia has claimed that Africans were impressed by the power of the colonizers. Their power manifested itself in locomotives, radios, bicycles, agricultural equipment.[1] They were irrefutable evidence of the colonizers' control over their environment. It is toward precisely this control that economic transformation is directed.

In the modern world, though, scientific and technological development necessary for such control requires certain minimum units of size.[2] It is very unlikely that the small islands in the Caribbean, for example, could individually develop diversified economies with reasonable standards of living. Such development can be achieved only through cooperation among a number of communities.[3] Lessons of the colonial past and realities of the present point to cooperation as a necessity.

The second requirement of the politics of transformation is, therefore, to develop, through patience and good will, techniques of cooperation among neighboring countries, whatever the differences they may have. Even so deeply divisive an issue as the boundary dispute between Venezuela and Guyana should not preclude cooperative efforts between Venezuela and the Caribbean countries.

In order to survive, small nations must seek to diversify not only their economies but also their contacts. The third requirement of the politics of transformation is the establishment of channels of communication with government, business, and intellectual centers in all the major in-

1. K. A. Busia, *Challenge of Africa* (New York: Praeger, 1962), p. 57.
2. See William Demas's excellent treatment of the subject in *The Economics of Development in Small Countries* (Montreal: McGill University Press, 1965).
3. An admirable example of such cooperation exists among the countries of Scandinavia.

13 THE POLITICS OF TRANSFORMATION

dustrialized countries of the world. Not only must nationals at home and abroad be fully informed of the objectives, problems, and strategy of the national government, but representatives of potentially sympathetic foreign governments should be kept equally informed of them.

The conduct of foreign governments often reflects, not national sentiments and aspirations, but merely the pressures and influences of powerful lobbies operating in their countries, and vested interests do not hesitate to apply these pressures upon the first hint of encroachment upon their activities. It is for this reason that the foreign policy of a democracy may be as imperialistic in its effects as that of a totalitarian regime. It is therefore essential that relations also be cultivated with influential countries, organizations, and institutions without interests likely to conflict with a developing country's efforts toward economic transformation.[4]

The fourth prerequisite of transformation is the need for people to identify with the political and economic objectives of the government. At every opportunity they must be shown exactly how various measures will benefit them in their daily lives. Leaders must encourage community and cooperative effort of every kind. They must rechannel into constructive fields energies previously dissipated in parochial jealousies and rivalries. Excellent examples of what this can achieve are the consumer cooperatives on the island of Tobago. The prime minister's Better Villages Program, a nationwide project of community self-help, is a project with great potential, even though it suffers perhaps from an atmosphere of personal patronage. An example of initiative at the party level was an Ideal Homes project begun by the Women's League in Tobago in the early years of the PNM. The objective was to demonstrate home improvement with simple and inexpensive materials and techniques.

The fifth requirement of the politics of transformation is freedom of discussion. This is the most valuable and fundamental freedom of all. It is also the first freedom that poses the most problems and gives rise to the greatest challenges and irritations. Inseparably bound ot it is the free use of the communications media. These are very often foreign-owned and controlled by interests not necessarily sympathetic to the objectives of the regime. The government is faced with the question of whether, in some circumstances, these media abuse the freedom by edi-

4. Admittedly, these may be somewhat hard to find.

torializing for the opposition. The demands for a better balance between news and opinion can lead to demands for control, especially if the media dismiss such demands as attempts to interfere with private enterprise and free speech.

Even complete state control of these media, however, need not be a result of interference with freedom of discussion depending upon whether the takeover occurs within the context of the politics of transformation or the politics of power. It is seldom easy to determine at the time of the event, for the politics of power often speaks in the language of transformation.

Whatever the mechanism of control, however, there should be legislative protection of the freedom to present varying points of view if there is the slightest chance that it will otherwise be subverted. The influence of the government, needless to say, should be on the side of the freedom rather than its control.

The many and serious difficulties involved in this issue of mass communication can be successfully approached only within the context of a public philosophy or national system of values. Such a system is part of the preamble to the Trinidad and Tobago Constitution. The society must commit itself to fundamental concepts of right and wrong, justice and injustice, racial peace, equality of opportunity, and the rule of law. In a society so committed, public opinion will itself exert pressure in the proper directions.

A more real danger to freedom of discussion may lie in the economic and institutional structure of the country and not require an overt attack in the manner of the politics of power. Where the vast majority of income earners are employees whose prosperity is tied to government policy, considerations of job opportunities and careers may exercise a powerful brake on freedom of discussion. The situation will be aggravated where a high level of unemployment prevails. In such circumstances, the law notwithstanding, freedom of discussion may be effectively curtailed by job or career manipulation by those who control political power. As the chilling of free speech is a prelude to further abuses of power, tendencies toward these conditions must be discerned and halted early in the process of transformation. In fact, the government must actively promote freedom of speech as a means of keeping open the lines of communication between the general public and those in power. Apart from the intrinsic benefits of the free circulation of ideas, there is no more powerful check on corrupt practices than freedom of expression.

The sixth and most important requirement of the politics of transformation is the political will to transform the society, and both leadership and the people must have it. This presupposes some knowledge of the risks involved, and in a system of collective or semicollective responsibility, it further presupposes a degree of uniformity of objectives sufficient to carry out long-range strategy and at least an equal degree of commitment to the strategy itself. Without these, the politics of power will emerge at the first sign of stress, and the strategy of transformation will be vitiated or abandoned.

In most ex-colonial countries, political will has already evolved by the time they achieve independence. It may have evolved through articulation of goals by leaders, generation of emotions, conditioning by protests and demonstrations, and commitment to sacrifice. In the period prior to independence, however, both the objectives and the people who stand in the way of them are easily identified. Political will is honed to a keen edge in the campaign; excitement is high, and the rank and file has a sense of continuous involvement. Discipline becomes easy to establish and maintain; it generates itself through the danger, the crisis, and the drama.

In the absence of rigorous conditioning of the population before independence is attained, independence itself becomes the climax, the high point of achievement and expectation. It becomes, not a stage in the process of growth or development or the means to an end, but an end in itself. And what follows becomes an inevitable anticlimax.

It is at this point that leadership has the choice of riding the wave of emotion or seeking to control it in anticipation of the greater journey ahead. If the leadership elects the former course, the future development will be all the more difficult. It will become necessary to resort to mass motivation. However, the most essential incentive to foster is the prospect of a new society free of the discouraging and irritating features of the old. Mass motivation produces only a shallow and temporary response. Enduring motivation is a product of a well-conceived mix of idealistic appeals and material rewards.

With proper motivation, the problem of discipline is a minor one, no different in kind or even degree from that in highly developed countries.[5] Greater problems are posed by the lack of educational institutions and industrial experience.

A weakening of the political will may arise if the difficulty of the problems of transformation are misjudged or if the task exceeds the political resources that can be mustered to it. This is often the case if the atmosphere allows external political constraints to come into play. Such constraints will result in frustration, bitterness, or apathy and lead eventually to instability.

Is transformation possible in the face of external economic or political pressure? There is as yet no definitive answer to this important question. It is the author's view, however, that it is possible within the context of the strategy outlined here. The task is a monumental one and can be accomplished only with maximum collaboration among the less developed countries. Success will also demand from the more developed countries far more enlightened policies than they have thus far been willing to establish.

By skillfully using a very special combination of favorable factors, an individual country here and there may be successful through only its own efforts, but the issue is very much in doubt for developed countries in general. An area with the potential for just such a favorable combination of factors is the Caribbean. Neutralizing these favorable conditons, however, are the area's political disunity and the proliferation of states, two matters that the following chapter will examine in detail.

Apart from the political problem of unification, the main problem confronting Caribbean countries, whose development has long depended on external capital, is the extent to which foreign corporations can fit into the perspectives and principles of national development plans. The experience of Trinidad and Tobago during its early years of independence can be of great significance in determining how far such harmony is, in fact, possible. The point may be further illustrated by the experience gained in three major steps in the program of transformation: regulation of the commercial banking system; the regulation of the insurance business; and the Finance Act of 1966, especially the

5. Witness the problems currently being experienced by the United Kingdom in her efforts to achieve industrial modernization and a favorable balance of payments.

changes in corporate taxation, the introduction of withholding taxes on payments abroad, and the negotiation of treaties to preclude double taxation. These matters were treated separately in a previous chapter.

ECONOMIC NEEDS

Equality of Opportunity

The drive toward self-government by ex-colonial countries is generally accompanied by the establishment of social justice and equality as essential political goals on the eve of independence. After independence, however, frequently these ideas conflict with the strategy of transformation. Clearly, there must be an interpretation of social justice and equality that is compatible with other political and economic goals. How, for example, can measures to restrict consumption and promote business expansion harmonize with the concepts of equality and social justice? Is inequality an inescapable characteristic of the growth and transformation process? Must philosophical and economic goals conflict?

No society has as yet achieved a system of completely equal rewards. Rewards will simply reflect the relative scarcity and value of the skills, capacities, and expertise that go into the productive process. In general, acquired knowledge and expertise have come to be of considerably more importance in the productive process than inherent capacities, and they represent a store of value and, consequently, capital.[6] The rewards for such knowledge and expertise are essentially for the effort that goes into acquiring them. If the rewards are too low, too few people will invest the effort. It may then be necessary to correct abnormal scarcities with abnormally high rewards.

Obviously, equality and social justice cannot mean equal rewards except for equal effort, and with equal effort, unequal scarcity may still result in unequal rewards. What is of paramount importance is that the system of rewards be determined, not in an arbitrary manner or on the basis of the most to the strongest, but on the basis of social goals. Society as a whole must determine rewards on the basis of its needs. And while the goals may remain constant, needs will vary over time; hence, there will be continual adjustments in the system of rewards.

6. Several writers within recent times have recognized the weaknesses in classifying all expenditure on education as social expenditure.

The program of incentives must have such a basis rather than the simplistic one that aims at attracting investment capital. Business expansion is the result of different kinds of people making different kinds of effort together and at different stages. Frustration at any stage of the effort, however strong the incentives at other stages may be, will slow down the whole process. Hence, a clear understanding of the kinds of effort that need encouragement is essential to any successful program of economic expansion.

It is now possible to examine the meaning of equality in this context:

First, all who are willing to make the effort must have available to them the opportunity of acquiring the necessary knowledge and expertise. This is the fundamental requirement of equality. The only limitation on this principle is society's needs in terms of numbers. There will, of course, be disparate levels of knowledge and expertise, and oversupply can be corrected by restricting selection to only the upper levels. This in effect rewards the greater effort.

Second, selection and advancement must be strictly by merit. Social, religious, or racial bias must be scrupulously avoided in all stages of the process.

Third, there must be recognition of the dignity of the human personality. This policy will keep physical characteristics from playing a part in advancement.

Fourth, disadvantaged groups that have suffered economic and educational prejudice must receive special compensatory attention. Social justice requires the establishment of human minimum levels of existence. There cannot be social justice, in conditions, say, of long periods of high unemployment. Also, any disproportionate burdens—for example, measures to restrain consumption—that weigh most heavily on the lower-income groups, should be offset by vigorous programs of social, economic, and cultural advancement.

These policies do not rest on sentiment. There are concrete philosophical, social, and economic reasons why equality and social justice must not be mere slogans or political propaganda, and the community at large must understand these reasons for any program of transformation to succeed. The need is all the more compelling where the traditional aim of political power was previously to advance the welfare of the few at the expense of the many.

The difficulties inherent in the process of economic transformation evoke questions not only of institutional development but of human development and leadership as well. Less developed countries face far more serious problems of economic growth than do developed countries, even more serious than developed countries faced at the pre-industrial stage. Paradoxically, although less developed countries can learn much from the techniques of countries that have developed successfully, their greatest problems stem from linkage of their economies to those of the developed countries and from the effects of the growing ease of communication on their populations. These two factors tend to relegate less developed countries to being merely the appendages of the highly developed ones and restrict their capacity to make the fundamental changes necessary to achieving their transformation goals.

Unemployment and Diversification

The most pressing social and economic problem in Trinidad and Tobago is unemployment, which for some years has remained a stubbornly constant 14 percent of the labor force. During that time, the national per capita income has almost doubled.

If the employment problem is to be solved, there must be considerable acceleration in the rate of diversification. Diversification requires, first, keeping national savings and the investment of savings within the country and, second, promoting savings by restraining consumption and providing financial institutions. The lower the rate of savings and investment, the greater the dependence on new injections of foreign capital; the greater the reliance on foreign capital, the greater the vulnerability to foreign influence.

Obtaining maximum employment and minimum external pressures requires generating the highest possible level of domestic savings, and there must be shrewd investment of these savings. This objective may be achieved by either incentives or regulations or, still better perhaps, a combination of both.

Fiscal incentives will usually enhance the attractiveness of capital investment in the domestic economy beyond the attractiveness of investment in neighboring states. Concessions must be reasonably generous, often at the risk of serious consequences to revenues and to the activities of the government. The tendency of these incentives is to expand the private sector while curtailing the government operations, at least in the short run, for lack of finance, at the very time when government must make a major effort to alleviate unemployment.[7]

Another effect of fiscal incentives is to further entrench an already exclusive business structure. The keystone of this structure is often the family corporation, whose management demands a minimum of expertise, whose hiring practices frequently feature sharp divisions along ethnic lines and whose dependency upon bank-overdraft financing is an all too common trait. Such enterprises tend to restrict themselves to areas of safe investment and to demand not only fiscal incentives but market protection as well.

The effects of these forces are to increase the government's reliance on fiscal policy with emphasis on indirect taxation (leading to higher consumer prices) and market protection (leading to still higher prices); to promote concentration of new domestic industries in safe areas of investment based on domestic demand—because the domestic market can be manipulated in their behalf—especially in consumer goods, which reinforces the consumption patterns of the colonial period and makes it even more difficult to redirect those patterns; and to divert resources into investment.

A whole series of measures may then result, some tending to neutralize others.[8] Basically, what is necessary is a complete departure from a pattern of consumption and rewards that has resulted in distribution of the national product by external rather than domestic directives. Given the responsibility of governments in the modern world to provide employment opportunities for all citizens in the labor market, a continuing high level of unemployment reflects either dependence on external influences, a lack of responsibility in the leadership, or both. Against a background of a continuing high rate of increase in the national income, it is even clearer that lack of external or internal responsibility is the basic cause of long-term high levels of unemployment.

Here it is not enough to examine what a developed country might do

7. The 1968-1973 Development Plan for Trinidad and Tobago estimates that about 25 percent of customs duty was forgone by the revenue in tax concessions between 1963 and 1967. The plan estimated that $17.3 million was forgone in 1967 and $10 million for the first six months of 1968.
8. Indirect taxation, market protection, and price control, for example, neutralize restrictions or consumer spending on articles produced under liberal tax concessions.

to solve the same problem. It is highly unlikely that a developed country would ever face the same kind of problem because it would never find itself in a condition of external control. To a developed country, the key to regulating employment is simply a matter of adjusting the business cycle; it can convert unemployment into inflationary pressures or inflationary pressures into unemployment. This is not so in the less developed country, where what is required is a full-scale assault on the whole problem of resource allocation. Such an assault requires regulating not only demand but consumption patterns and income levels as well.

Domestication of Foreign Firms

Control of resource allocation is indispensable to resource mobilization. If resource allocation is determined by external influences that are not amenable to domestication, the level of employment becomes irrelevant to the decision-making process and to that extent reflects the lack of responsibility of decision makers to the domestic population. The classic response of some reformers is to nationalize. Nationalization does not, however, solve the problem of markets. Although this technique may work in such economies as those of Russia and China, it probably will not work where the lines of production bind the economy to foreign trade. And this is the position of most countries whose goal is transformation.

Nationalization is, of course, one means of transferring foreign ownership to local ownership, in this case, ownership by the state. Even so, nationalization is not a definitive step to local control, for problems of management, financing, and marketing may display problems of ownership. Except to free-enterprise dogmatists, there is nothing intrinsically wrong with nationalization. The manner and terms of nationalization can, however, be of great consequence. There must be fair treatment for those who may be subject to the exercise of state power; this requires the establishment and acceptance of ground rules to govern cases involving the property of foreign nationals. These rules should by convention be binding on all states that accept them, and they should also be enforceable by international tribunals.

Pending transformation of the economy, what is necessary is usually not nationalization but domestication. The principal issue then becomes a matter of how far domestication can go. Domestication of the foreign firm is an attempt to induce it to accept the same obligations as a domestic owner. This means basically sympathy with and acceptance of the social and economic goals of the host country. The most difficult problems arise from international corporations carrying on business in more than one foreign country. These are usually integrated operations, and their various parts can hardly be treated separately. Nevertheless, because the profitability of the operations in each country will eventually have to be wrestled with by the tax authorities, there should be at least a rough method of apportionment. Apart from employment policies, especially the matter of employing nationals in senior positions, the principal issue will be the use of profits. On the one hand, foreign shareholders are entitled to dividend distributions on their investment; on the other, the distribution of profits is a matter of as much concern to the state as any other form of resource allocation. Anything but voluntary cooperation by the foreign firm is likely to fail. A foreign firm that feels threatened will mobilize support quite effectively by raising the specter of diminishing foreign investment. Domestication can have the prospect of success only when carried out by a strong nationalist government and only in the absence of a general policy of socialization or nationalization.

In general, the degree to which domestication can succeed will depend on the extent of foreign investment. The greater the extent (in proportion to domestic investment), the more difficult the task and the smaller the benefits. Nevertheless, domestication as an alternative to nationalization must, in general, remain a major policy objective.

Hence, the principal argument in favor of economic integration in the Caribbean, for example, is that it will offer greater scope for both ownership and domestication of business within the area. Fragmentation tends to reduce each political unit's effectiveness in controlling its economy. Whether within such a framework domestic entrepreneurship can develop to adjust the imbalance with foreign ownership is a question closely related to the previous one.

Promoting Domestic Enterprise

The promotion of domestic entrepreneurship is a major prerequisite for economic transformation, though the methods employed vary from country to country. Two principal factors are involved: first, the extent of preindependence development of a dependable core of local businessmen with the experience and conviction to drive into new fields, especially manufacturing; and, second, the extent to which this group of businessmen is representative of the community at large or has indicated the ability to identify with the broader interests of the population.[9] These factors are usually more complex in ex-colonial countries with ethnically diverse populations and historical backgrounds of favoritism toward particular ethnic groups.

The major problem is how to correct the bias without disrupting the existing degree of harmony or doing violence to principles of justice that must underlie the new society. Where an ethnic minority dominates the business sector, a government may, out of economic necessity, find itself facing the forbidding prospect of having to deploy its newly gained equalizing power in such a way as to bolster further a position of already unfair advantage and exacerbate the very tensions it was entrusted to abolish. This is the most compelling reason for opening up the business structure to participation.

It is an extraordinary fact that most ex-colonial governments have committed themselves to economic transformation and place high priority on economic growth and the performance of the private sector; but rarely is there the slightest provision for preparation in business techniques and organization. There is not yet an appreciation that business, like law, medicine, history, economics, and theology, can be taught in schools or in adult education programs. The old European tradition of on-the-job training for management prevails with barnacle-like tenacity.

Even worse than a lack of training facilities is the tendency in the public sector to refuse to apply the principles of organization, management and personnel administration that the advanced countries have developed with vast success over the past fifty years. As public corporations operate some of the largest enterprises, the public sector's neglect of training in business methods and management reinforces the widely held view—a view propagated by private enterprise dogmatists—that public enterprises are by definition inefficient. The assault on the prob-

9. The situation is vastly different from that described by Pierre Uri in relation to the European Economic Community. See his paper "Foreign Investment: The European Experience" in *Multinational Investment in the Economic Development and Integration of Latin America* (Inter-American Development Bank, 1968), pp. 257 ff.

lem of management and entrepreneurship must begin in the educational system and the public sector, particularly in public utilities and the other service enterprises. In fact, except perhaps in pricing policies, public enterprises should be the common ground between the public and the private sectors, providing personnel for both and recruiting personnel from both, and they should have an even more comprehensive and imaginative training program. The idea that business competence is hereditary or can be picked up at random is as valid as the same argument with regard to competence in engineering, medicine, or law.

A more difficult problem than training is that of gaining solid business experience. A great deal is possible in this direction in the public sector, but there can be appreciable results only if planning includes the private sector. Techniques for accomplishing this purpose are not difficult to find. Governments, which themselves spend so much on services, forgo large revenue sums, and impose such sacrifices on the population to influence capital investment, can influence recruitment policies in key areas of the private sector.

The government must lay down guidelines for recruitment and, in some cases, promotion policies; it should create machinery of its own, such as a review board to assure implementation. It can apply sanctions of one kind or another as a last resort, after persuasion has failed. The central difficulty is to make available sufficient numbers of trained people and then to assure them of opportunities for experience and advancement. Most governments can accomplish this goal for nationals in general but do not go nearly far enough to promote equality of opportunity among nationals, particularly in the private sector.[10]

The effort to promote equality of opportunity is wholly justifiable, not only as a benefit in itself but also on historical grounds and perhaps even more so as a counterweight to the unequalizing effect of the program of industrialization by incentives: those who pay for maintaining the system are due the repayment of a place within the system. But this means that nationals, from whatever racial or cultural background, can gradually prepare themselves to replace the foreign entrepreneurs and managers.

10. Such programs should take into account the special position of nationals who are discriminated against or in some way disadvantaged for historical causes or on ethnic or other grounds.

Complications arise when large international firms claim the right to maximize personnel efficiency by interchange of staff, and special account must be taken of their needs. They can, however, be required to demonstrate that they are fitting nationals into a personnel policy that accommodates their training needs and puts them on an equal footing with their foreign counterparts.

This hardly seems too severe a demand of corporations that for long periods enjoyed almost unrestricted control of their affairs and that even now enjoy many advantages unavailable to them at home. To be sure, they deserve the fruits of their investment and effort, but the argument that well-trained local nationals make less skillful managers than foreigners seems an empty one in light of the management policies they practice in their own countries.

Daniel Guérin, after a visit to the Caribbean in 1960, said, "History seems to have led it into an impasse where, such is our initial impression, it seems to have slight chance of working its way out."[1]

Many others, pursuing the same point, have observed that the real barriers have been artificial ones—linguistic, monetary, and commercial —and these were the barriers that were the means of achieving vertical integration with the metropolitan power. Mail traveled from Kingston to Port-of-Spain via London during most of the colonial period. Until 1878, Tobago had more contact with the United Kingdom, nearly two thousand miles away, than it had with Trinidad, eighteen miles away. There were simply no means for regional interests to assert themselves. Territorial governors in Caribbean colonies dealt directly with the secretary of state for the colonies rather than through local or regional channels. The entire fabric of the colonial system not only tolerated insularity but actively promoted it. By the middle of the twentieth century— when colonial powers for a variety of reasons were no longer able to maintain their overseas systems—self-contained nationalism had become so much the order of the day that newly independent former colonies, already preconditioned to isolation, could not help but view federation skeptically. Federation, with its frequent demands of local sacrifice to federal interests, seemed to many of these new states to be little more than another form of colonialism. And if African and East Asian examples of federation difficulties were inadmissible on the grounds of newness, one could gather equally telling testimony in Wales, Quebec, and the Ukraine.

THE MICROSTATE AND THE MINISTATE

The recent blossoming of small Caribbean states has brought under examination the concepts of nationhood, independence, and self-determination after a period in which the validity of these concepts had eluded criticism. One of the major products of the anticolonial movement has been the almost universal acceptance of the right to self-government. However, as the colonial powers established the boundaries of their conquests with little regard for cultural or ethnic considerations, some of their former possessions that have acquired independence come close

1. Daniel Guérin, *The West Indies and Their Future* (London: Dobson, 1961), p. 9.

14 THE FUTURE OF THE CARIBBEAN

to fitting H. G. Wells's somewhat cynical description of a nation as "any assembly, mixture, or confusion of people which is either afflicted by, or wishes to be afflicted by, a foreign office of its own."[2]

While this is really only nationalism's negative side, negative emotions can be just as powerful as positive ones. In fact, most instances of nationalism will be found to have been simply the consequences of rejection of the imperialist system. In Asia and Africa, the anticolonial movement's essential impulse was the struggle to escape the inherent inequality of colonial status.

In most of Asia and Africa, however, the positive impulses of collective pride, historical background, ethnic affinities, and cultural identity soon prevailed and permitted formulation of the goals of economic and social progress.

Lately, however there has emerged a new kind of small nation-state whose impulse is predominantly negative. Its inhabitants, though perhaps willing, cannot find others with whom they feel they can associate. There is also the small state in which the negative and positive impulses are more or less in balance. The first can be called the microstate and the second, the ministate.[3] An example of the former is Anguilla, and an example of the latter is Trinidad and Tobago—both in the Caribbean. These are also states that recognize the severe limitations of smallness and separateness. They are the anomalies of the international community.

The international community has confined itself to concern for international relations of these states, notably to the issue of membership and voting rights in the United Nations.[4] Our principal interest in such states, on the contrary, is to consider to what extent the mechanics of independence is applicable to them.

William Demas has pointed out that in the past size alone was not an insurmountable obstacle to economic growth, citing such examples as

2. H. G. Wells, *An Outline of History* (London: Cassell, 1961), p. 982.
3. The differentiation is made because the ministate is now acceptable fashion in the international community. The microstate is not.
4. There have been excellent papers on the subject by Roger Fisher of Harvard University and Patricia Wohlgemeth Blair. See Patricia Blair, "The Mini-State Dilemma," Occasional Paper No. 6 (New York: Carnegie Endowment for International Peace, October, 1967); see also Roger Fisher, "The Participation of Micro-States in International Affairs," an address to the American Society of International Law on April 26, 1968.

Switzerland, Luxembourg, Denmark, New Zealand, Norway, and Sweden.[5] Patricia Blair has selected the figure of 300,000 as the upper limit for the microstate (which she describes as "a mini-territory"). There are obvious difficulties of terminology, which both authors identify and tackle. The crucial issue in the matter is the nature of the linkage between the economy of the micro- or ministate and the external world.

There is no assumption here that transformation is necessarily the desirable goal. The nature of the small state's relationship with the external world and the goals of those who inhabit it will determine whether and to what extent it accepts and applies the economics of independence. The real issue is whether it will be possible to achieve the transition even if the state accepts the strategy.

The economics of independence for small countries generally moves in the direction of economic integration, which itself thus becomes part of the pattern of transformation. The advantage of integration through geographical proximity is that it tends to promote a more viable economic and political structure. And though political independence may be accompanied by economic dependence, political independence is an essential prerequisite to the economics of independence, and the concepts of political independence and nationhood do not really apply to the microstate. As Roger Fisher has pointed out, "Islands like Samoa, Nauru, and Anguilla, even if they govern themselves, will be quite unlike larger nation-states."[6] The problem of the microstate is, fundamentally, a philosophical one: Can people regard themselves as free if they feel constrained to occupy a position of inequality or dependence?

Caribbean leaders, like those in Africa, have often lamented the systematic fragmentation of their area. In each case, the resulting political divisions have made economic cooperation difficult and economic transformation even more difficult. Political fragmentation tends to deny the peoples of underdeveloped countries the benefits of modern science and technology, for the outlay of capital and skilled personnel is often beyond the resources of any single small state. For some of the more ambitious economic and scientific projects being planned, the resources of even the larger nation-states are inadequate. The process is

5. William Demas, *Economics of Development in Small Countries* (Montreal: McGill University Press, 1965).
6. Fisher, "The Participation of Micro-States in International Affairs."

clearly developing in such techniques as "economic integration," "complementarity," and "multinational investment." The difference between the new and the old colonial integration is the difference between equality and inequality.

How do Samoa, Nauru, and Anguilla fit into the picture? Can they be left to their own devices, or must someone come to their assistance, and if so, who? One solution is that a larger state might oversee them as protectorates or wards, but this implies the position of inequality so much a part of the colonial relationship. A second possible solution is the provision of assistance and advice by a department of the United Nations, as suggested by Roger Fisher. However, this entails delicate problems of criteria for such services, not to mention the question of interference in the internal affairs of states.[7] This is an area that the United Nations must not enter except for the purpose of conciliation and provided that parties to any dispute request its services.

A distinction should perhaps be made between the case where the right to separation is challenged by interested parties and where a separate identity is a universally acknowledged fact. Where the right to separation is challenged, the international community should use its influence through its various instruments and organizations to bring about reconciliation. In the case of Anguilla, this should have been the responsibility of the United Kingdom. Anguilla, it should be noted, is a micro-unit within a ministate that is still a dependency of the United Kingdom, and it is clear that Anguilla would have chosen continued association with Britain after separation from St. Kitts and Nevis if this course had been open to that island.

The truth is that the Anguilla issue reflects the weakness of the entire Caribbean area. The withdrawal of colonial authority has not been succeeded by the establishment of any other effective authority, and the Caribbean has become a spectacle of tiny states floundering about in the sea. It is a volatile area with a low flash point, whose potential instability makes it susceptible to economic frustration, external intervention, and fratricidal disputes of the kind that has recently erupted between Guyana and Venezuela.

7. *Ibid.*

FORCES AT WORK

The patterns of transformation in Trinidad and Tobago lead naturally to the question of the future of the entire Caribbean area. However, even the concept of a Caribbean area is nebulous. Certainly it does not include Mexico, but does it necessarily exclude the other countries of Central and South America that border on the Caribbean? More common usage does exclude them, and in this sense the Caribbean area is almost synonymous with the West Indies. But the term "West Indies" is itself imprecise and often excludes the Greater Antilles—Cuba, Jamaica, Puerto Rico, and Hispaniola.

The Caribbean area as conceived in this chapter includes not only the Greater and Lesser Antilles and the Bahamas but also the mainland South American territories of the Caribbean. The area is obviously not one of tidy definitions. For some four and a half centuries it was—and in many places is—dominated by colonial power of one kind or another.

Within recent times, the area has come increasingly under the shadow of the United States, which during the present century has resorted to various sorts of intervention in the Caribbean and Central America. The United States also has possessions in the Virgin Islands, so, apart from the mainland territories, the Caribbean area today comprises a Dutch West Indies, a French West Indies, a British West Indies, and a United States West Indies as well as the independent countries such as Cuba, Haiti, the Dominican Republic, Jamaica, Trinidad and Tobago, and Barbados. Consequently, the Caribbean area is merely a geographical expression. Adding to the confusion, the entire area falls within the province of the Monroe Doctrine and the various glosses placed on that doctrine from time to time by different presidents of the United States.

Most of the islands are very small communities, ranging from a few inhabitants in some of the Bahamas and the Grenadines to over 8 million in the largest island, Cuba. The islands are also highly diverse in ethnic composition, cultural heritage, language, and political institutions. There are republics (Cuba, Haiti, the Dominican Republic), monarchies (the formerly British territories), dictatorships, and parliamentary democracies based on the Westminster model. There are independent countries, colonies, "overseas departments," and "associated states."

Emancipation brought no substantive changes to the social and economic structure in the Caribbean. Generally the system of production continued in the tradition of the plantation, even though cocoa, coconuts, and citrus may have replaced sugar and cotton in some places, just as free labor replaced slave labor. Yet, if the colonial plantation system was unacceptable and if modifications of it were unproductive, what was the answer?

To the advocates of a modernized agriculture as the solution to the area's economic ills, Arthur Lewis warns that the reinvigoration of agriculture means taking more people off the land if a reasonable standard of living is to be achieved for those who remain.[8] With the growing population of the region, alternative avenues of employment still had to be found. This pointed inescapably to the need for industrialization.

The plantation pattern continued until the early fifties when, with growing democratization, many of the states adopted programs of industrialization by incentives (mainly to foreign capital) modeled on the Puerto Rican system. In Trinidad and Tobago and later in Jamaica, the program was known as the aid-to-pioneer-industries legislation. Later Cuba embarked upon a Marxist process of radical transformation through highly centralized planning. The rest of the Caribbean has continued to proceed by modifying the existing structure. Adopting the techniques that it did, the Cuban regime chose to move out of the free-enterprise system, leaving unanswered the question of whether the colonial plantation-type economy can be dismantled and a modern industrial economy constructed simultaneously within a framework of private enterprise. With growing disenchantment over the Puerto Rican model, the question has become even more urgent.[9]

Apart from the formidable problems of transportation even in the larger islands, many of the smaller islands, or microstates, have little prospect of modernization except through tourism and foreign capital in real estate development. This course leads eventually to a landless and underprivileged indigenous population, to domination by external influences, and to the establishment of power centers with at best a

8. W. Arthur Lewis, "Industrial Development in the Caribbean," *Caribbean Economic Review* (Trinidad: Kent House, 1951).
9. For a penetrating critique of the Puerto Rican model, see Lloyd Best's "Chaguaramas to Slavery?" *New World Quarterly* (Jamaica), vol. 2, no. 1 (1965), pp. 43-70.

limited sense of responsibility to the people of the island.

Weak political authorities, hard put to provide employment for a growing labor force, are not likely to be able to withstand the pressures of investors offering quick returns. Inexperienced administrations can fall prey to superficially beneficial propositions. High prices may need to be paid in terms of liberal fiscal and other concessions to avoid political embarrassment. Permissiveness toward gambling casinos, exclusive clubs and beaches, drug sanctuaries, smuggling dens, and underworld havens can become a standard technique of attracting capital. The need for "development capital" may take precedence over social values.

In such circumstances, the Havana of Batista can become the model for the microstate rather than the present Cuban or Puerto Rican example. Nor are the larger islands likely to escape these influences once they are fully established in the area.

There is no intent here to imply that integration by itself will bring about economic transformation. As Havelock Brewster and Clive Thomas point out, even advocates of integration often base their arguments on "a logic which is not more convincing than that of intuitive generalizations and dubious clichés." Such arguments

. . . include the views that the gains from internal free trade would be significantly large; that a customs union would ensure the advance of industrialization; that integration is concerned only to a minor extent with agriculture, that collectively the West Indian territories would secure very large economies of scale; that resources would be used more efficiently; that all territories would share in the total gains of integration.[10]

Here the union between Trinidad and Tobago is a highly relevant example. Not only did Tobago fail to derive any economic benefit from the union with Trinidad, but in fact the union was, for a considerable period, an actual handicap to the smaller island. A conceptual error sometimes arises from confusing the structure of government with its philosophy. The assumption is that a structure favorable to development implies a governmental philosophy of development, and the benefits of the structure alone are exaggerated. Correspondingly, such a view underrates the importance to entrenched conservatism of a develop-

10. Havelock Brewster and Clive Y. Thomas, *The Dynamics of West Indian Economic Integration* (Jamaica: Institute of Social and Economic Research, University of the West Indies, 1967), p. 7.

ment philosophy of concession. Even while the mechanism of change is being assembled, there are forces working to wreck it.

Claudio Veliz has remarked how, in Latin America, the middle classes have maintained and even strengthened the traditional structure, leading some of the major countries into situations of institutional stability and economic stagnation. "Far from reforming anything," says Veliz, "they have become firm supporters of the Establishment; they have not implemented significant agrarian or fiscal reforms but have displayed remarkable energy trying to become landowners or to marry their off-spring into the aristocracy."[11]

In Chile, particularly, a high degree of concentration of economic power and the association of the higher bureaucracy with industrial and financial groups brought the state increasingly under the control of private interests. "The State," says Osvaldo Sunkel, "the main instrument of economic and political power, grown large and influential as a result of the initiative of left-wing parties, has, in this way, become an instrument for the preservation of the status quo rather than for the promotion of structural change.[12]

Thus the real purpose of the mechanism of change may be frustrated even while it is being assembled, or the mechanism may itself be rendered ineffectual by the conversion of a philosophy of change into one of conservatism. The strategy of transformation may itself be transformed into the politics of survival.

THE CASE FOR UNITY

The single most essential requirement to bring about the transformation necessary for Caribbean progress is political union. The most compelling reason for union can be made simply by stating its alternatives: dissipation of domestic resources, domination by external interests, and economic and social frustration.

These are not future alternatives to be averted at a leisurely pace over the coming years: these are the current conditions besetting the Caribbean. Anguilla and Barbuda are not anomalous curiosities; they are the

11. Claudio Veliz, *Obstacles to Change in Latin America* (London: Oxford University Press, 1965), p. 2.
12. Osvaldo Sunkel, "Change and Frustration in Chile," in *Obstacles to Change in Latin America* (London: Oxford University Press, 1965), pp. 135-136.

predictable and inevitable results of fragmentation that can and will arise elsewhere in the absence of corrective action.

Nor will size or past stability be proof against breakdown. By Caribbean standards certainly, Trinidad and Tobago enjoyed an enviable position in many respects. Yet witness the jarring emergency that began in that country in April 1970 and may turn out to be only the opening round of a series of emergencies.

The solution—and it is not a simple one within easy reach—lies in uniting the communities of the Caribbean in either a federation or a unitary state. Unfortunately, the reaction to either kind of union tends too often to be visceral rather than cerebral. The possible variations of unitary statehood especially have been unexplored. A study of the possibilities ought to take into account the valuable experience gained in the case of Trinidad and Tobago, current conditions notwithstanding. It is lamentable that an area so rich in cultural and political forms has been unable to work out a suitable political framework for meeting its special requirements.

Culturally, the Caribbean islands and British or formerly British mainland territories are mainly Afro-European, with a submixture of Latin and Anglo-Saxon influences. In Trinidad and Tobago and Guyana, of course, further diversification arises from East Indian immigration. The islands are thus a natural point of convergence among Anglo-Saxon, North American, and Latin American peoples, as well as among Europeans, Asians, and Africans. Diversity has produced a cultural texture rich in physical form, language, music, and customs. Yet this vast resource of cultural potential has remained largely untapped, at least partly because of the introversion that comes of isolation. The intermingling resulting from union could provide the springboard for a cultural regeneration that would hardly fail to enhance social perspectives and elevate social values.

Nowhere else perhaps is the natural and the beautiful so confluent with the artificial and the repugnant. George Lamming, in his *Pleasures of Exile* pilloried the cultural alienation of leaders lost in the fantasy of their ceremonial English upper-class dress. Vidia Naipaul in his *Middle Passage* and *The Mimic Man* ridiculed the irrelevance, the arrogance, the spiritual alienation, and the intellectual superficiality of the middle class.

Even these flaws are in part traceable to isolation. Certainly union could not help but correct some of them; for with exposure to variety comes comparison, and with comparison comes selectivity and rejection.

The economic advantages of union that have been enumerated earlier in this work will not be repeated here except to note that the various aspects of integration have been the subjects of a growing body of literature on the subject, the most significant being a series of studies recently undertaken by the Institute of Social and Economic Research, University of the West Indies.[13]

Even with acceptance of the wisdom of integration, there remains the question of what degree of integration to pursue. No doubt, because of the recognition of the risks involved in transformation, the universalistic approach to economic integration in the Caribbean[14] came for a time to be more popular than the sectoral or partial approach. *The Economics of Nationhood*, for example, saw the problem as follows:

> Barbados will not unify with St. Kitts or Trinidad with British Guiana or Jamaica with Antigua. They will be knit together only through their common allegiance to a central government. Anything else will discredit the conception of Federation and, in the end, leave the islands more divided than before.[15]

Hence, as Brewster and Thomas observe, "the prevailing conception is undoubtedly that the choice is between a universalistic type of association or none at all."[16]

Basic to any fruitful argument about economic integration in the Caribbean area must be the realization that the existing political-economic system is untenable. With this awareness, there is room for either a universalistic or a partial approach for one or another group of territories and its relations with the rest. Given the necessary political will, it may even be that the most successful approaches do not fit into such restrictive categories. The first attempt at unification of the British islands

13. "Studies in Regional Economic Integration," *Social and Economic Studies*, Institute of Economic and Social Research, Mona, Jamaica: G. L. Beckford and M. H. Guscott, "Intra-Caribbean Agricultural Trade," vol. 2, no. 2; G. L. Beckford, "The West Indian Banana Industry," vol. 2, no. 3; Norman Girvan, "The Caribbean Bauxite Industry," vol. 2, no. 4.
14. See Brewster and Thomas, *West Indian Economic Integration*, pp. 2-4.
15. *The Economics of Nationhood* (Trinidad: Government Printing Office, 1959), p. 11.
16. Brewster and Thomas, *West Indian Economic Integration*, p. 4.

ended in failure largely because of the inability to dovetail economic necessity with political reform. The experience demonstrates that an overview is essential to harmonizing initiatives in specific fields.

As a matter of tactics, it may be prudent to keep the more general approach in the background, because of the negative effects of the ill-directed former federation's initiatives and the present need to show beyond any doubt the value of each sectoral initiative. However, the tactics of the campaign are one thing, and the strategy of the war is another. There is still widespread approval of some degree of collaboration in economic and other matters, but considerable differences exist over the goals and methods of the collaboration. In this regard, the sectoral approach clearly emerges the superior.

A strategy of action must take into account not only factors such as sentiment and political motivation but also a whole range of other variables to ensure that the strategy is itself not subverted by the growth of rapid institutional and other self-reinforcing obstacles to change. Here, as elsewhere, the vicious circle emerges in the problems of developing nations.

Perhaps the greatest danger that faces the Caribbean in the process of uniting is that circumstances do not permit a leisurely approach. There is the immediate crisis in the microstate; and the ministates are being increasingly and almost irresistably attracted to the economic and political power of extraregional corporations and governments. Even the larger states, such as Cuba, Haiti, and the Dominican Republic, are susceptible to this attraction, which is in utter conflict with the goals of the integration process.

The fundamental requirement of a new order is consequently political. No order can succeed if it is based on existing constitutional arrangements, which in effect serve only to veil the political vacuum left by the withdrawal of imperial power. The inescapable demands of the new order are the following:

First, the remaining outposts of empire in the guise of overseas departments and associated states must be liquidated.

Second, the peoples of the area must assume responsibility for planning their destiny.

Third, the major Western powers must recognize their responsibilities and express them in a plan of assistance for the region.

Fourth, there must emerge one political entity of the eastern Caribbean islands and Guyana as the first step toward union of all the British or former British territories.

Fifth, the boundary dispute between Guyana and Venezuela must be settled once and for all.

These are the irreducible minimum requirements of a rational framework for the new dispensation that the Caribbean so desperately needs. Other possible developments would be the following: the extension of the Caribbean Free Trade Association area to include the other independent territories; discussions between the new political grouping and the remaining independent states with a view to political union of all the islands; and, finally, economic integration with either the Central American Common Market or Latin American Free Trade Association countries.

Among the courses open to the peoples of the Caribbean are the integration just outlined, collaboration with the Communist bloc along Cuban lines, or reversion to colonial dependence—this time on the United States.

The people of the Caribbean will not freely choose the third course; it would simply be the chaotic consequence of failure of the other alternatives. As to the question of the choice between the first two, it will depend partly upon the character of the policies of the major external powers that exercise influence in the area.

The second course is not mentioned as the threat of a vague sort of blackmail intended to produce instant and massive aid to keep the area from "going Communist." It is simply a possibility that must be recognized. Just after Batista's downfall there were those who accurately predicted Cuba's future course, and they were called alarmists. The fact is that Cuba does offer an alternative, and however unpalatable it may be to others, that alternative will undoubtedly be probed if other avenues prove impassable.

Aid is needed, of course, but this does not mean large amounts of money. What the area needs is largely assistance in acquiring the skills of technical and industrial management, more equitable terms of trade, fairer interest rates, and the like. The Caribbean will also need understanding of and sympathy for its goals of transformation. Perhaps most important, the Caribbean will require of the major powers a policy of restraint. They must resist internal pressures to resort to dollar diplomacy to enforce the often mistaken policies of their powerful corporations. And they must restrain themselves from interfering in the internal political affairs of Caribbean communities, however much they disagree with the conduct of those affairs or the results they may bring about. To a small nation there is really no such thing as a friendly giant; there are only giants who look where they walk and giants who do not.

However beneficial, the assistance and good offices of the major powers will not, of course, suffice alone. The success or failure of the Caribbean will be a matter for us in the Caribbean to determine. We must awake to the fact that the Caribbean crisis is not around the corner; it is upon us. Around the corner may be chaos.

We of the Caribbean are as much the masters of our own destiny as we choose to be. With firm political will, we can put an end to that part of the unfortunate conditions that we ourselves have created, and the major part of those we have have inherited; as we do so, others may see the wisdom of doing the same.

A decade ago we witnessed the futility of halfhearted union. Now we are experiencing the futility of separateness, however purposeful. To seize and maintain the better future that can be ours, we must impel ourselves toward purposeful union. We must build one nation of the Caribbean in our own likeness.

I, THE KING

Whereas by my instructions of the 3rd September, One Thousand Seven Hundred and Seventy-Six, to Don Manuel Falquaz, Captain of Foot, who was then appointed Governor of my Island of Trinidad to Windward; and by the Commission which I afterward gave Don Joseph de Abalos, appointing him Intendent-General of the Province of Caracas, I thought proper to establish regulations, and to grant various privileges for the population and commerce of the said Island; I have no resolved, on the representation of the said Intendent, and at the instance of certain colonists already established in the said Island, and others who request permission to settle therein, to establish complete instructions in the following articles:

Article 1st.

All foreigners, the subjects of powers and nations in alliance with me, who are desirous of establishing themselves, or who are already settled, in the said Island of Trinidad, shall sufficiently prove to the Government thereof, that they are of the Roman Catholic persuasion, without which they shall not be allowed to settle in the same; but the subjects of these my dominions, or those of the Indies, shall not be obliged to adduce such proof, because no doubt can arise as to their religion.

Article 2nd.

All foreigners who shall be admitted, agreeable to the foregoing article, to reside in the said Island, shall take, before the Governor thereof, the oath of fealty and submission; by which they shall promise to obey the laws and general ordinances to which Spaniards are subject; and immediately there shall be granted to them, in my Royal name, gratuitously for ever, the lands proportionally mentioned according to the following rules.

Article 3rd.

To each white person, of either sex, four fanegas and two sevenths; and the half of that quantity of land for each Negro or coloured slave, which the settlers shall induce; the lands to be so distributed, that everyone may participate of the good, middling and bad; the assignments of lands to be entered in a book of registry, with insertion of the name of each settler, the day of his or her admittance, the number of individuals composing his or her family, their rank, and from whence they came; and copies of such entries shall be given to them, to serve as titles to their property.

Article 4th.

Free Negroes and coloured people, who, as planters and heads of families, establish themselves in the said Island, shall have one-half of the quantity of land as is above assigned to the white, and the same portion for each slave they introduce, the proper documents to be given to them, as to the whites.

Article 5th.

When the settlers shall have resided five years in the said Island, and bound themselves to an entire residence therein, they shall receive all the rights and privileges of naturalization, as likewise their children, whether brought by them to the Island, or born therein; and consequently shall be admitted to all honourable public employments and to posts in the militia according to their respective capacities and circumstances.

Article 6th.

That no capitation money or personal tribute, however small, shall be imposed upon the inhabitants at any time, save and except the annual sum of one dollar for each Negro or coloured slave, to be paid after a ten years' residence in the said Island; and that the said proportional sum shall never be augmented.

Article 7th.

During the first five years of residence, the Spanish and foreign settlers shall have liberty to return to their countries or former places of abode; in which case they shall be allowed to take from the said Island, all the goods and property by them introduced into the same, without paying any duties upon exportation; but may pay for all property acquired by them during their residence in the said Island, the sum of 10%. It is to be well understood, however, that the lands which shall have been assigned to such settlers, who afterwards voluntarily quit the Island, shall devolve to my Royal patrimony, to be given to others, or disposed of as shall appear to me most fit.

Article 8th.

I grant to the former and recent settlers who, not having necessary heirs, make by last will and testament a disposition of their property, the power of bequeathing their estate to their relations or friends wherever they may be; and if these choose to settle in the said Island, they shall enjoy the privileges granted to the persons whom they succeed; but if they prefer withdrawing the property from the said Island, they may do so, upon paying 15% upon the whole by way of a duty on exportation; that is, if the testator has lived more than five years in the said Island; and if the residence of the testator has been within that period, they shall pay only 10% as is provided in the last article. And the fathers, brothers and sisters, or relations, of those who die intestate, shall succeed without any diminution to their estate, provided that they are Catholics, and domiciled in the said Island, even should they be settled in foreign countries, and if they should not be able, or do not wish to be enrolled among the inhabitants of the said Island, I do hereby give them permission to dispose of the property of the successions by sale or cession, according to the rules laid down in the foregoing article.

Article 9th.

I do also give permission to all settlers, who, according to the Spanish law, have the disposition by testament or otherwise of their real property, to bequeath the same, if it does not admit of a convenient division, to one or more of their children, provided the legal portions of the others, or that of the widow of the testator, be not injured thereby.

Article 10th.

Any settler who, by reason of any lawsuit, or other just and pressing motive, may require to go to Spain, to any other province of my Indies, or to foreign dominions, shall request permission from the Governor, and obtain the same, provided it be not an enemy's country, or to carry away property.

Article 11th.

Spanish and foreign settlers shall be free from payment of tithes, or 10% on the produce of their lands for ten years; and after that period (to be computed from the first day of January, 1785) they shall only pay half tithes, that is, 5%.

Article 12th.

They shall also be free for the first ten years from the payment of the Royal duty of alcabala on the sales of their produce and merchantable effects; and shall afterwards only pay an equivalent for the said duty of 5%; but whatever shall be embarked for these Kingdoms in Spanish vessels shall be forever exempt from any duty on exportation.

Article 13th.

As all the inhabitants should be armed even in time of peace, to keep the slaves in subjection, and resist any invasion or the incursion of pirates; I do hereby declare that such obligation is not to render them responsible to the duties of a regular militia, but they are only to present their arms for inspection, in review before the Governor, or some officer appointed by him every two months; but in time of war, or an insurrection of the slaves, they shall assemble together for the defence of the Island, in such way as the Commander-in-Chief hereof may direct.

Article 14th.

All vessels belonging to the former or recent settlers, whatever may be their tonnage or make, shall be carried to the said Island and enrolled therein, and the proofs of the property in them enregistered, upon which they shall be accounted Spanish vessels; as also such vessels as may be acquired from foreigners by purchase, or other legal title, until the end of the year One Thousand Seven Hundred and Eighty-six; the said vessels to be free from the duty paid in qualifying foreign vessels for the Spanish trade. And such as wish to build vessels in the said Island shall have free access to the woods required by Government; save and except those which may be destined for the building of vessels for the Royal Navy.

Article 15th.

The commerce and introduction of slaves into the said Island shall be totally free of duties for the term of ten years, to be reckoned from the beginning of the year One Thousand Seven Hundred and Eighty-five, after which period the colonists and traders in slaves shall only pay 5% on their current value at the time of their importation; but it shall not be legal to export slaves from the said Island to any other of my Indian dominions. without my Royal permission, and the payment of 6% of their importation into other of my dominions as aforesaid.

Article 16th.

The said settlers shall be permitted, having first obtained a licence from the Government, to go to the islands in alliance with me, or the neutral ones to procure slaves, either in vessels belonging to or freighted by them, being Spanish bottoms; and to export for the payment of the said slaves, the necessary produce, and property, on payment of 5% on exportation; the said duty to be paid by the trader in slaves who, with my permission, imports them to the said Island, besides the duty on their entry; from all which I have freed the settlers, in order to excite agriculture and commerce.

Article 17th.

The intercourse of Spain with the inhabitants of Trinidad, and the exportation of licensed produce from the said Island to my American islands and dominions shall be entirely free of all duties for the space of ten years, to be reckoned from the first day of January, One Thousand Seven Hundred and Eighty-five, at the expiration of which time, all the articles which are exempted by the last article of free commerce from payment of duties on entry into these Kingdoms, shall likewise be free, nor shall any more impositions be levied than those which the productions of my other West India Dominions are liable to.

Article 18th.

All Spanish and foreign merchandise, and the wine, oil, and spirituous liquors, the produce of these my Kingdoms, which shall be entered and exported to the said Island, shall be free of all duty for the said term of ten years, and shall also be introduced and circulated therein free of duty, but are not to be exported therefrom to any of my other Indian dominions, but if they should be permitted to be exported therefrom, for any urgent or just cause, such permission shall only extend to Spanish goods, and that on payment of the duties fixed by the said article of free commerce.

Article 19th.

In order to facilitate every means by which the population and commerce of the said Island can be increased, I do hereby permit, for the said term of ten years (to be computed from the beginning of the year One Thousand Seven Hundred and Eighty-five) all vessels belonging to the same, or to my subjects in Spain, to make voyages to the said Island with their cargoes directly from those ports of France where my Consuls are resident, and to return directly to the said ports with the fruits and produce of the said Island, except money, the exportation whereof by that route I absolutely prohibit; subject however to the following obligation, on the part of the said Consuls, which is not to be dispensed with: that they shall draw up a particular register of everything embarked, and sign, seal, and deliver the same to the care of the captain or

master of the vessel so that he may present the same to the officer charged with the receipt of my Royal Revenues in the said Island of Trinidad; and subject likewise to the payment for the introduction of the goods and merchandise into the said Island, of the sum of 5%, and the same amount on such produce as shall be exported from the same, and carried to France, or to any foreign port, without touching at any one of the Spanish ports which are licensed to trade with the Indies.
Article 20th.

In case of urgent necessity (to be attested by the Governor) I do hereby grant to the inhabitants of the said Island, the same permission as is contained in the foregoing article, under the precise condition that the captains or masters of the vessels do make accurate invoices of their cargoes, and deliver the same to the proper officers in the said Island; so that by comparing the said invoices with the goods imported, the said duty of 5% may be levied on the then current value of the said goods at the said Island of Trinidad.
Article 21st.

In order that the former and recent inhabitants may be furnished with the most necessary supplies for their maintenance, their industry and agriculture, I have given the most stringent orders to the Commander-in-Chief of the province of Caracas, to purchase on account of my Royal revenue, and transport to the said Island, horned cattle, mules and horses, to be delivered to the said settlers at first cost, until such time as they have sufficient stock to supply themselves.
Article 22nd.

I have likewise given the same order for the supplying the said Island with flour and meal for the term of ten years; and that, if, by any accident, a scarcity should take place, the Governor shall permit the inhabitants to go with their own vessels, or those of others of my subjects, to the foreign islands to purchase what they stand in need of; and for that purpose to export such produce as may be necessary, paying on exportation the sum of 5%, and the same proportion on the flour and meal imported into the said Island.
Article 23rd.

I have likewise ordered that all matters and things of the manufacture of Biscay and the rest of Spain, which may be required by the settlers for their agricultural pursuits, shall be imported into the said Island,

and given to the settlers at prime cost for the said term of ten years; but after that period, each person must provide himself, and if during that period there be an urgent necessity for these matters and things, the settlers shall be allowed to procure them from foreign islands belonging to the Powers in alliance with me, subject to the same duties as the flour and meal.

Article 24th.

I have likewise ordered that two secular or regular priests, of known erudition and exemplary virtue, and skilled and versed in foreign languages, shall be appointed to reside in the said Island to serve as new parish priests to the settlers, and I shall assign to them the necessary stipends to enable them to live in the decent manner which their character requires, without being any charge on their parishioners.

Article 25th.

I permit former and recent settlers to propose to me, through the medium of the Governor, such ordinances as shall be most proper for the regulating the treatment of their slaves and preventing their flight; and at the same time, to point out such rules as the Governor shall observe relative to this article, and the reciprocal restitution of fugitive slaves from other islands belonging to foreign powers.

Article 26th.

I also enjoin the said Governor to take the utmost care to prevent the introduction of ants into the island, which have done so much injury in the Antilles; and for that purpose, to cause the equipage and effects of the settlers arriving at the said Island to be severally examined; and as the inhabitants are the persons most interested in the execution of this order, they shall propose to the Government two of the most active and proper persons to examine the vessels, and zealously watch over the observance of this point.

Article 27th.

When the crops of sugar become abundant in the said Island of Trinidad, I shall allow the settlers to establish refineries in Spain, with all the privileges and freedom from duties which I may have granted to any natives or foreigners who shall have established the same; and I shall allow in due time the erection of a Consular Tribunal to increase and protect agriculture, navigation and commerce; and I have charged the Governor in his private instructions, and the other judges of the said

Island, to take care that all the inhabitants, Spaniards and foreigners, be well and humanely treated, and justice equitably administered to them; so that they may not meet with any molestation or prejudice, which would be greatly to my Royal displeasure.

Article 28th.

Lastly, I grant to the former and recent settlers the privilege whenever they have questions to ask me worthy of my Royal consideration, of directing their representations to me through the medium of the Governor and the Chief Secretary of States for the Indies; and if the matters are of that nature that require a person to be sent on their account, the inhabitants shall request permission to that effect and I will grant the same, if just.

And that the articles contained in this Ordinance be duly carried into effect, I grant a dispensation from all laws and regulations contrary to them, and I command my Council of the Indies, and the chanceries and audiences thereof, Presidents, Captains-General and Commanders-in-Chief, Ordinary Judges in the ports of France, to keep, fulfil and execute, and cause to be kept, fulfilled and executed, all the rules and regulations contained in this my Cedula. Given at the Royal Palace of San Lorenzo, on the twenty-fourth day of November, One Thousand Seven Hundred and Eighty-three, sealed with my privy seal, and countersigned by my Secretary of State and of the general administration of the Indies, undersigned.

(Signed) I THE KING
(Countersigned) Joseph de Galvez.

Source: The Trinidad Historical Society Publication No. 108.

TOBAGO

The Secretary of State's despatch and Royal Order in Council constituting Tobago a Ward of Trinidad

In continuation of Council Paper No.[1]

Registered No. of Correspondence No. 4533/1898.

THE SECRETARY OF STATE TO THE GOVERNOR

Trinidad

Downing Street
1st November, 1898.

Sir,

I have the honour to transmit to you copies of an Order of Her Majesty in Council dated the 20th of October, 1898, revoking the Order in Council of the 17th November, 1888, uniting the Colonies of Trinidad and Tobago, except clauses 1, 2, and 37, and revoking the Order in Council of the 6th of April, 1889, amending the same, and providing that the Island of Tobago shall be a Ward of the Colony of Trinidad and Tobago.

I have etc.,
J. Chamberlain.

AT THE COURT OF BALMORAL
The 20th day of October, 1898,

Present:

THE QUEEN'S MOST EXCELLENT MAJESTY
Duke of Fife
Earl of Kintore
Lord George Hamilton

1. Original is unnumbered.

WHEREAS, by an Order of Her Majesty in Council, bearing date the seventeenth day of November, 1888, hereinafter called the principal Order, the Colony of Trinidad and its dependencies, and the Colony of Tobago, were, from and after the first day of January, 1889 (in the said Order referred to as "the appointed day"), united into one Colony:

And whereas by Our Order in Our Privy Council, bearing date the 6th day of April, 1889, We did amend the 18th Clause in the principal Order:

And whereas it is expedient to revoke the principal Order, except Clauses 1, 2 and 37 thereof, and to revoke the Order in Council of the Sixth day of April 1889:

NOW THEREFORE, in pursuance of the powers in Us vested by the Trinidad and Tobago Act, 1887, it is hereby ordered by Her Majesty, by and with the advice of Her Privy Council, as follows:—

1. The whole of the principal Order, except Clauses 1, 2 and 37, and the Order in Council of the Sixth day of April 1889, are hereby revoked, but such revocation shall not affect the validity, invalidity, or effect of anything done or suffered before the date of the coming into force of this Order.

2. On and after the date of the coming into force of this Order, the Island of Tobago shall be a Ward of the Colony of Trinidad and Tobago; and the revenue, expenditure, and debt of Tobago shall be merged in and form part of the revenue, expenditure, and debt of the united Colony, and the debt due from Tobago to Trinidad shall be cancelled.

3. Save as in and by this Order expressly otherwise directed the Laws of Trinidad in force on the date of the coming into force of this Order shall be in force in Tobago, and the Laws therefore in force in Tobago, so far as they differ from the Law in force in Trinidad, shall thereupon cease to be in force. Provided that this clause shall not affect the validity, invalidity, or effect of anything done or suffered before the date of the coming into force of this Order, or any right, title, obligation, or liability acquired or incurred before that date.

4. All future Ordinances enacted by the Legislature of the Colony shall extend to Tobago. Provided that the Legislature of the Colony may at any time by Ordinance provide for the special regulation of all or any of the matters and things dealt with in the several Acts, Ordinances, and Regulations of Tobago enumerated in the Schedule hereto,

and of any other and further matters and things in respect of which it may be deemed necessary to enact special and local Ordinances or Regulations applicable to Tobago as distinguished from the rest of the Colony.

5. The Acts, Ordinances, and Regulations of Tobago enumerated in the Schedule hereto shall, until repealed or amended by the Legislature of the Colony, continue locally in force in Tobago, but such Acts, Ordinances, and Regulations shall in every case be construed as amended by and read together with this Order; and in particular wherever in such Acts, Ordinances, and Regulations any duty is imposed or power conferred upon any specified officer or person, such duty or power shall be performed or exercised by such person or persons as the Governor may from time to time by Proclamation appoint for the purpose.

6. Until the Legislature of the Colony shall otherwise provide, the following provisions shall take effect in Tobago, that is to say: —

(a) Any land tax payable in respect of lands in Tobago shall be levied at such rate as to the Governor in Council shall seem fit, notwithstanding that any similar tax is levied throughout the rest of the Colony at a higher rate.

(b) The license fees authorized by "The License Regulation 1893," shall continue to be collected and paid in Tobago as heretofore in lieu of any license fees in force in the rest of the Colony, save and except that no license fees shall be payable for the keeping of horses, geldings, mules, mares, and asses.

(c) The license fees for spirit licenses now payable in Tobago shall continue to be collected and paid as heretofore, the Trinidad Ordinance No. 1 of 1881 to the contrary notwithstanding.

(d) There shall not be charged upon produce which shall have been raised or manufactured in Tobago, and shall be shipped from Tobago for ports or places beyond the limits of the Colony, any taxes, rates, or charges for raising funds in aid of immigration.

7. Such of the powers and duties heretofore exercised and performed by the Commissioner of the Supreme Court in Tobago, and by the Deputy-Marshal of Tobago, as it shall seem expedient to continue, shall be exercised and performed by such person or persons as by rules of the Supreme Court, to be framed under the Trinidad Judicature Ordinance, 1879, shall be prescribed and determined.

8. This Order shall come into force from and after a date to be proclaimed in Our Colony of Trinidad and Tobago by Our Governor and Commander-in-Chief of Our said Colony.

A. W. Fitzroy

SCHEDULE

1. The Stamp Ordinance, No. 19 of 1879.
2. The Vaccination Ordinance, 1882, No. 3 of 1882.
3. The Medical Aid Ordinance, 1882, No. 6 of 1882.
4. The Turtle Preservation Ordinance, 1885, No. 2 of 1885.
5. The Wild Birds Protection Ordinance, 1885, No. 8 of 1885.
6. The Anglican Church, Incorporated Trustees Ordinance, 1887, No. 7 of 1887.
7. The License Regulation, 1893, No. 2, of 1893, as amended by the Amending Licenses Regulation, 1893, No. 6 of 1893.
8. The Destitute Persons Relief Regulation, 1893, No. 10 of 1893.
9. The Liquor License Ordinance, 1883, No. 1 of 1883, as amended by the Amending Liquor License Regulation, 1893 (No. 7, 1893), and by the Amending Liquor License Regulation, 1894, No. 10 of 1894.
10. An Act relating to Lands in this Island commonly called the Three Chains, 28 Vict. cap. 1, as amended by Regulation No. 5 of 1894.
11. The Road Regulations, 1894, No. 3 of 1894, as amended by the Road Amendment Regulation 1894, No. 6 of 1894.

Source: *Trinidad Royal Gazette*, December 8, 1898.

Chapter I, Section 1,[1] of the Constitution illustrates the liberal philosophy that permeated the document. The philosophy enshrined in the Constitution, as well as the social and political ideas embodied in it, is further illustrated in the preamble, which reads as follows:

Whereas the People of Trinidad and Tobago
(a) have affirmed that the nation of Trinidad and Tobago is founded upon principles that acknowledge the supremacy of God, faith in fundamental human rights and freedoms, the position of the family in a society of free men and free institutions, the dignity of the human person, and the equal and inalienable rights with which all members of the human family are endowed by their Creator;
(b) respect the principles of social justice and therefore believe that the operation of the economic system should result in the material resources of the community being so distributed as to subserve the common good, that there should be adequate means of livelihood for all, that labour should not be exploited or forced by economic necessity to operate in inhumane conditions but that there should be opportunity for advancement on the basis of recognition of merit, ability and integrity;
(c) have asserted their belief in a democratic society in which all persons may, to the extent of their capacity, play some part in the institutions of the national life and thus develop and maintain respect for lawfully constituted authority;
(d) recognize that men and institutions remain free only when freedom is founded upon respect for moral and spiritual values and the rule of law;
(e) desire that their Constitution should enshrine the above-mentioned principles and beliefs and make provision for the protection in Trinidad and Tobago of fundamental human rights and freedom; . . .

Thus the Constitution is a complete repudiation of authoritarian rule. The concept of democracy that it embodies is based on the rule of law and on fundamental human rights and freedoms. Religious influence on the society is reflected in an acknowledgment of the supremacy of God, and the reference to "the position of the family in a society of free men and free institutions" in particular draws its inspiration from the philosophy of the Catholic Church.

Ideas of "social justice" and "the common good" reflect the influence of social democratic thought and indicate that the framers of the Constitution were not hidebound by sterile eighteenth-century liberalism.

1. "The Recognition and Protection of Human Rights and Fundamental Freedoms."

APPENDIX 3
THE INDEPENDENCE CONSTITUTION, 1962

The philosophical guidelines are sufficiently clear to ensure public commitment to freedom. They indicate the goals of government legislation and social action, but no attempt has been made to outline the means by which the goals must be achieved. Even the goals themselves are, in the context of the Constitution, persuasive only. They are in the preamble, and not the operative sections.

The remaining principal characteristics of the Constitution are as follows:

1. It is a written constitution. As such it is subject to interpretation by the courts. The courts usually will intervene, however, only when there is an actual or threatened interference with some right. The citizen may then ask for a declaration of his rights or for an injunction to restrain the offending authority from violation of his rights. The courts will not intervene to determine an academic question of interpretation.

2. It is a unitary constitution, that is, one based on the supremacy of one parliament. There may be two parliaments in the unitary state but one or other must be the supreme legislative authority. In case of conflict, it is that authority which prevails.

3. It embodies a constitutional monarchy, with the queen of the United Kingdom as sovereign, but she is sovereign in her right as queen of Trinidad and Tobago, and not of the United Kingdom.

This is one of the more difficult concepts to understand. The queen of the United Kingdom is, in fact, only nominally queen. She is represented in Trinidad and Tobago by a governor-general who, for all practical purposes, is the constitutional monarch in Trinidad and Tobago with powers and functions severely circumscribed by the Constitution.

The first point to observe about the governor-general is that he is appointed by the queen of the United Kingdom but only on the advice of the prime minister of Trinidad and Tobago.

The second point is that, except in a few matters specifically prescribed, the governor-general acts only on the advice of the cabinet. As Section 63(1) of the Constitution prescribes,

The Governor-General shall, in the exercise of his functions, act in accordance with the advice of the Cabinet or a Minister acting under the general authority of the Cabinet, except in cases where by the Constitution or any other law he is required to act in accordance with the advice of any person or authority other than the cabinet. . . .

Cases in which the governor-general may act on "his own deliberate judgment" are as follows:

(a) The appointment of a prime minister. Under Section 58(1),

(i) such an appointment must be of a member of the House of Representatives who is the leader of the party that commands the support of the majority of the members, or

(ii) if it appears that the party does not have an undisputed leader or that no party commands the support of such a majority, the member of the House of Representatives who, in his judgment, is most likely to command the support of the majority of members of that House and who is willing to accept the office of prime minister.

(b) The appointment of a person to act for the prime minister in the latter's absence or illness and when his advice cannot be obtained or on the prime minister's disqualification from being a member of the House of Representatives.

(c) Appointment and removal of the leader of the opposition. Here the governor-general is required to appoint the leader in the House of Representatives of the party that commands the support of the largest number of members of the House in opposition to the government. The governor-general may revoke the appointment where the leader of the opposition ceases to command the support of a majority.

(d) Signification of approval for an appointment to his personal staff.

4. It is patterned on the Westminster model. Corresponding to king, Lords, and Commons, there is a governor-general, a Senate, and a House of Representatives. There are, however, no hereditary peers, and knights do not have the right to sit in either house. The Senate consists of twenty-four members appointed by the governor-general as follows:

(a) Thirteen on the advice of the prime minister,

(b) Four on the advice of the leader of the opposition,

(c) Seven on the advice of the prime minister after consultation with religious, economic, or social bodies or associations.

The minimum age qualification is thirty years, and citizenship is a requirement.

A senator's seat becomes vacant if the governor-general, acting on the advice of the prime minister or leader of the opposition, as appropriate, so declares. It also becomes vacant on the next dissolution of Parliament after his appointment. Other instances where a senator vacates his seat are in case of absence for a prescribed number of sittings, nomination as a candidate for election to the House of Representatives or election thereto, cessation of citizenship, conviction for prescribed offenses, proof of being of unsound mind, or if declared bankrupt.

The Senate is presided over by a president, in whose absence the vice-president presides. There is also provision for temporary senators.

Any bill, except a money bill, may be introduced in the Senate. A money bill sent one month before the end of the session to the Senate and not passed within that month may be assented to by the governor-general. Any other bill rejected by the Senate in two successive sessions after having been sent at least one month before the end of each session becomes law on assent by the governor-general.

Special constitutional provisions relate to taxation and expenditure bills and those compounding or remitting the public debt. All such bills must signify the approval of the cabinet.

The House of Representatives comprises thirty members or such number as may be provided for by order under Section 54 of the Constitution. At least two members must be from Tobago. The speaker presides and may be a person elected from outside the membership of the House.

The general direction and control of the government resides in the cabinet, which is collectively responsible to Parliament. The cabinet consists of the prime minister, the attorney general, and such other ministers as may be appointed. The governor-general assigns ministerial portfolios on the advice of the prime minister.

The Constitution embodies the traditional division of governmental functions into executive, legislative, and judiciary. The Supreme Court of Judicature is headed by the chief justice, who is appointed by the governor-general on the advice of the prime minister.

The court consists of a high court and a court of appeal. Judges other than the chief justice are appointed by the governor-general on the advice of the Judicial and Legal Service Commission. Judges vacate office on attaining the age of sixty-two years. A judge may otherwise be removed from office if the Judicial Committee of the Privy Council in the United Kingdom so advises. Referral to the Privy Council can arise only after investigation by a tribunal appointed by the governor-general on the advice of the prime minister after consultation with the Judicial and

Legal Service Commission. Pending the determination of the matter, the governor-general may, on the advice of the chief justice, suspend the judge whose conduct is being investigated.

Appeals from the Court of Appeal are rightfully made to the Judicial Committee of the Privy Council in the following cases:

(a) From final decisions in civil proceedings where the matter in dispute is of the value of $1,500 and upward, or where the dispute involves directly or indirectly a claim to or question regarding property or a right of the value of $1,500 and upward.

(b) Final decisions in proceedings for dissolution or nullity of marriage.

(c) Final decisions in any proceedings involving interpretation of the Constitution.

(d) Other cases prescribed by Parliament.

In addition, the Court of Appeal may itself grant leave of appeal to the Judicial Committee of the Privy Council in the following cases:

(a) Where by reason of the great general or public importance of the matter or otherwise, the court considers that such leave should be given.

(b) In such other cases as may be prescribed by Parliament.

While the independence of the judiciary is secured by the Legal Service Commission, the protection of the civil service is sought through the Public Service Commission, which controls appointments and promotions except to the highest offices (over which the prime minister possesses a power of veto).

One further aspect of the Constitution that is of considerable importance involves the conduct of elections. To assist in free and impartial elections, two commissions are provided for under the Constitution—a Boundaries Commission and an Elections Commission. Both commissions consist of a chairman and not less than two or more than four members, appointed by the governor-general on the advice of the prime minister. The appointment in every case is for a fixed term of five years.

Removal from the Boundaries Commission may follow disqualification (as by being a minister, parliamentary secretary, senator, member of the House of Representatives, or public officer) or mental or physical disability or misbehavior. Such removal is by the governor-general on the advice of the prime minister.

In the case of the Elections Commission, the removal procedure is similar to that applicable to a judge, except that there is no reference to the Judicial Committee of the Privy Council in the United Kingdom.

BOOKS

Alford, C. E. R. *Island of Tobago*. Dorchester, England: Longmans, Green, 1956.

Almond, Gabriel A., and Coleman, James S. *The Politics of Developing Areas*. Princeton, N.J.: Princeton University Press, 1960.

Altamira, Rafael. *A History of Spain*, translated by Muna Lee. Princeton, N.J.: Van Nostrand, 1949.

Apter, David E. *The Politics of Modernization*. Chicago: University of Chicago Press, 1965.

Asturias, Miguel A. *The President*, translated by Frances Partridge. London: Gollancz, 1963.

Augier, F. R.; Gordon, S. C.; and Hall, D. G. *Making of the West Indies*. London: Longmans, Green, 1960.

Ayearst Morley. *The British West Indies*. London: Allen & Unwin, 1960.

Bell, Wendell, and Oxaal, Ivor. *Decisions of Nationhood: Political and Social Development in the British Caribbean*. Denver, Colo.: University of Denver, 1964.

Brewster, Havelock, and Thomas, Clive Y. *The Dynamics of West Indian Economic Integration*. Jamaica: Institute of Social and Economic Research, University of the West Indies, 1967.

Brown, Michael Barratt. *After Imperialism*. London: Heinemann, 1963.

Burns, Sir Alan. *History of the British West Indies*. New York: Barnes and Noble, 1965.

Busia, K. A. *The Challenge of Africa*. New York: Praeger, 1962.

Carmichael, Gertrude. *History of the West Indian Islands of Trinidad and Tobago, 1498-1900*. London: Ridman, 1961.

Craig, Hewan. *The Legislative Council of Trinidad and Tobago*. London: Faber & Faber, 1952.

Dass, M. N. *The Political Philosophy of Jawaharlal Nehru*. London: Allen & Unwin, 1961.

de Linaje, Veitia. *Norte de la contractión de las Indias Occidentales*. Seville, 1672. (English translation by John Stevens. *The Spanish Rule of Trade for the Indies*. London: 1702.)

Demas, William G. *The Economics of Development in Small Countries*. Montreal: McGill University Press, 1965.

de Verteuil, L. A. A. *Trinidad*. London: Cassell, 1884.

Easton, David. *The Political System*. New York: Knopf, 1963.

Fraser, L. M. *History of Trinidad*, 2 vols. Trinidad: Government Printery, 1856.

Guérin, Daniel. *The West Indies and Their Future*. London: Dobson, 1961.

Gunasekera, H. A. *From Dependent Currency to Central Banking in Ceylon.* London: G. Bell and Sons, 1962.

Hayes, C. J. H. *Nationalism.* New York: Macmillan, 1960.

Hicks, J. R. *Essays in World Economics.* Oxford: Clarendon Press, 1959.

Hobbes, Thomas. *Leviathan.* Oxford: Blackwell, 1957.

Hollis, Sir Claude. *Brief History of Trinidad under the Spanish Government.* Trinidad: Government Printery, 1961.

Hoyos, Fabriciano. *Rise of West Indian Democracy.* Barbados: Advocate Press, 1963.

James, C. L. R. *Life of Captain Cipriani,* Nelson Lancs., England: Coulton, 1932.

Kennedy, John F. *Strategy of Peace.* New York: Harper, 1960.

Lamming, George. *Pleasures of Exile.* London: Joseph, 1960.

Lenin, V. I. *Imperialism.* London: Martin Laurence, 1934.

Lewis, Gordon K. *The Growth of the Modern West Indies.* London: MacGibbon & Kee, 1968.

Lewis, W. Arthur. *Politics in West Africa.* London: Allen & Unwin, 1966.

———. *The Theory of Economic Growth.* London: Allen & Unwin, 1955.

Lipset, Seymour. *Political Man.* London: Heinemann, 1960.

Lloyd, Peter J. *International Trade Problems of Small Nations.* Durham, N.C.: Duke University Press, 1968.

London, Kurt, ed. *New Nations in a Divided World.* New York: Praeger, 1963.

Lynch, John. *Spanish Colonial Administration, 1782-1810.* London: Athlone Press, 1958.

Mboya, Tom. *Freedom and After.* London: André Deutsch, 1963.

Meikle, L. S. *Confederation of the British West Indies vs. Annexation to the United States of America.* London, 1912.

Merivale, H. *Lectures on Colonialization and Colonies, Delivered before the University of Oxford in 1839, 1840, and 1841.* Oxford: Oxford University Press, 1928.

Mill, J. S. *On Liberty.* London: Oxford University Press, 1948.

Millikan, Max, and Blackmer, Donald L. N., eds. *The Emerging Nations.* Boston: Little, Brown, 1961.

Mordecai, John. *The West Indies.* London: Allen & Unwin, 1968.

Myrdal, Gunnar. *Asian Drama,* 3 vols. New York: Twentieth Century Fund, 1968.

———. *Beyond the Welfare State.* New York: Bantam, 1967.

Naipaul, V. S. *The Middle Passage.* London: André Deutsch, 1962.

———. *The Mimic Man.* London: André Deutsch, 1967.

Nehru, Jawaharlal. *The Discovery of India.* London: Meridian, 1951.

———. *Toward Freedom.* Boston: Beacon Press, 1958.

Nkrumah, Kwame. *Autobiography.* Edinburgh: Thomas Nelson, 1957.

———. *Ghana.* Edinburgh: Nelson, 1957.

———. *I Speak of Freedom.* London: Heinemann, 1961.

O'Loughlin, Carleen. *Economic and Political Change in the Leeward and Windward Islands.* New Haven, Conn.: Yale University Press, 1968.

Ottley, C. R. *Complete History of the Island of Tobago in the West Indies.* Trinidad: Guardian Commercial Printery, n.d.

Oxaal, Ivor. *Black Intellectuals Come to Power.* Cambridge, Mass.: Schenkman, 1968.

Pannikar, K. M. *The Afro-Asian States and Their Problems.* London: Allen & Unwin, 1959.

Parry, J. H., and Sherlock, Phillip. *A Short History of the West Indies.* London: Macmillan, 1960.

Plato. *Dialogues,* translated by W. H. D. Rouse. New York: New American Library, 1956.

Preiswerk, Roy, ed. *Regionalism and the Commonwealth Caribbean.* Trinidad: Institute of International Relations, 1969.

Prest, A. R. *A Fiscal Survey of the British Caribbean.* London: HMSO, 1957.

Pye, Lucian. *Communications and Political Development.* Princeton, N.J.: Princeton University Press, 1963.

Pye, Lucian, and Verba, Sydney, eds. *Political Culture and Political Development.* Princeton, N.J.: Princeton University Press, 1965.

Robertson, Sir Dennis H. *Britain in the World Economy.* London: Allen & Unwin, 1954.

Robinson, E. A. G., ed. *The Economic Consequences of the Size of Nations.* London: Macmillan, 1960.

Roll, Eric. *A History of Economic Thought.* London: Faber & Faber, 1953.

Salmon, C. *Caribbean Confederation.* London: Cassell, 1888.

———. *Depression in the West Indies.* London: Cassell, 1884.

Singham, A. W. *The Hero and the Crowd in a Colonial Polity.* New Haven, Conn.: Yale University Press, 1968.

Stalin, Josef. *Marxism and the National and Colonial Question.* London: Lawrence & Wishart, 1942.

Suárez, Andrés. *Cuba: Castroism and Communism, 1959-1966.* Cambridge, Mass.: M.I.T. Press, 1967.

Thomas, Alfred B. *Latin America: A History.* New York: Macmillan, 1956.

Thomas, John Jacob. *Froudacity.* London: Unwin, 1889.

Touré, Sékou. *La Guinée et l'Emancipation Africaine.* Conakry, Guinea: Impr. Nationale, 1959.

Toynbee, A. J. *The World and the West.* London: Oxford University Press, 1952.

Veliz, Claudio. *Obstacles to Change in Latin America.* London: Oxford University Press, 1965.

Wellisz, Stanislaus. *The Economics of the Soviet Bloc.* New York: McGraw-Hill, 1966.

Wells, H. G. *An Outline of History.* London: Cassell, 1961.

Williams, Eric. *Capitalism and Slavery.* London: André Deutsch, 1964.

———. *Documents of West Indian History, 1492-1655.* Trinidad: PNM Publishing, 1963.

———. *History of the People of Trinidad and Tobago.* London: André Deutsch, 1964.

———. *The Negro in the Caribbean.* Washington, D.C.: Associates in Negro Folk Education, 1942.

Woetzel, Robert K. *The Philosophy of Freedom.* Dobbs Ferry, N.Y.: Oceana Publications, 1966.

Woodcock. H. I. *History of Tobago.* Ayreshire Express Office, England: Smith & Grant, 1887.

PAMPHLETS

"Annexation of Chaguaramas." Trinidad: Government Printery, 1963.

Blair, Patricia. "Mini-State Dilemma." Occasional Paper No. 6. New York: Carnegie Endowment for Peace, 1967.

Bullbrook, J. A. "Aborigines of Trinidad." Trinidad: Royal Victoria Institute, 1960.

Lewis, J. O'Neil. "A Comparison of the Economic Development of Trinidad and Jamaica and of Puerto Rico during the Fifteen Years from 1939 to 1953." B.Litt. dissertation, Oxford University, 1957.

Lewis, Sir W. A. "Agony of the Eight." Barbados: Government Printery, 1965.

Ottley, C. R. "An Account of Life in Spanish Trinidad, 1498-1797." Trinidad: College Press, 1955.

Poyntz, J. "Present Prospects of the Famous and Fertile Island of Tobago." London, 1683.

"Refutation of the Pamphlet Colonel Picton Lately Addressed to Lord Hobart." London: John Stockdale, 1805.

Robinson, A. N. R. "Fiscal Reform in Trinidad and Tobago." Trinidad: PNM Publishing, 1966.

Robinson, A. N. R., *et al.* "The Party in Independence." Trinidad: PNM Publishing, 1965.

Springer, H. "Reflections on the Failure of the First West Indian Federation." Cambridge, Mass.: Center for International Affairs, Harvard University, 1962.

GOVERNMENT REPORTS

Annual Statistical Digest. Trinidad and Tobago: Central Statistical Office, 1967.

British Caribbean Federation. *1956 Conference Report.* Trinidad and Tobago: Government Printery, 1956.

———. *1953 Plan.* London: HMSO, 1957.

———. *Report by the Conference Held in London in February 1956.* Cmd. 9733. London: HMSO, 1956.

British Caribbean Standing Closer Association Committee. *Report, 1948-1949.* Bridgetown: Advocate Co., 1949.

Budget Speeches. *Hansard Reports, 1962-1967.* Trinidad and Tobago: Government Printery.

Commission of Enquiry into the Oil Industry of Trinidad and Tobago. *Report.* London: André Deutsch, 1964.

Commission on Trinidad and Tobago Disturbances, *Report,* 1937. Cmd. 5641. London: HMSO, 1938.

Crown Union Commission. *Report.* Cmd. 4383. London: HMSO, 1933.

Documents Relating to the Bases Leased to the United States of America. *Gazette Extraordinary,* vol. 127, no. 83. Trinidad, 1958.

Draft Third Five-Year Development Plan, 1969-1973. Trinidad and Tobago: Government Printery, 1968.

Draft Third Five-Year Development Plan, 1969-1973, Trinidad and Tobago, Preliminary Comments. Trinidad and Tobago: Chamber of Industry and Commerce, March 31, 1969.

Eastern Caribbean Federation Conference Report, 1962. London: HMSO, 1962.

Economics of Nationhood. Trinidad and Tobago: Government Printery, 1959.

Financial Statistics. Trinidad and Tobago: Central Statistical Office, 1967/1968, 1968/1969.

Foreign Relations of the United States, 1941, vol. 3. Washington: U.S.

Government Printing Office, 1959.

Hansard Reports, Trinidad and Tobago, vol. 1, 1961-1962; vol. 1, part 1, 1962-1963; vol. 2, 1962-1963; vol. 3, 1963-1964; vol. 4, 1964-1965; vol. 6, 1965-1966; vol. 7, 1966.

Moyne, Lord. *West India Royal Commission Report.* Cmd. 6607. London: HMSO, 1945.

Multinational Investment in the Economic Development and Integration of Latin America. Washington, D.C.: Inter-American Development Bank, 1968.

National Income of Trinidad and Tobago, 1952-1962. Trinidad and Tobago: Central Statistical Office, 1962.

"Report of His Majesty's Commission of Legal Inquiry on the Colony at Trinidad" (no. 551). Great Britain, *Parliamentary Papers* (Commons), 1826-1827, vol. 23, p. 883.

Royal Commission Appointed in December 1882 to Enquire into the Public Revenue Expenditure, Debts and Liabilities of the Islands of Jamaica, Grenada, St. Vincent, Tobago and St. Lucia, and the Leeward Islands. *Report.* Cmd. 3840. London: HMSO, 1884.

Second Five-Year Development Plan, 1964-1968. Trinidad and Tobago: Government Printery, 1963.

Tobago Planning Team Report. Trinidad: Colonial Development and Welfare, 1957.

Trinidad and Tobago, Independence Constitution Joint Select Committee. *Proposals.* Trinidad: Government Printery, 1962.

Wood, E. F. L. *Report on His Visit to the West Indies and British Guiana, December 1921 to February 1922.* Cmd. 1679. London: Great Britain Colonial Office, 1922.

JOURNALS

Beckford, G. L. "Studies in Regional Economic Integration: The West Indian Banana Industry." *Social and Economic Studies,* Institute of Economic and Social Research, University of the West Indies, vol. 2, no. 3 (Mona, Jamaica, 1967).

Beckford, G. L., and Guscott, M. H. "Studies in Regional Economic Integration: Intra-Caribbean Agricultural Trade." *Social and Economic Studies,* Institute of Economic and Social Research, vol. 2, no. 2 (Mona, Jamaica, 1967).

Best, Lloyd. "Chaguaramas to Slavery?" *New World Quarterly,* vol. 2, no. 1 (Jamaica, 1965), pp. 43-70.

Girvan, Norman. "Studies in Regional Economic Integration: The Caribbean Bauxite Industry." *Social and Economic Studies,* Institute of Economic and Social Research, University of the West Indies, vol. 2, no. 4 (Mona, Jamaica, 1967).

Lewis, W. Arthur. "Industrial Development in the Caribbean." *Caribbean Economic Review* (Trinidad: Kent House, 1951).

McIntyre, Alister. "Some Issues of Trade Policy in the West Indies." *New World Quarterly*, vol. 2, no. 2 (Jamaica, 1966), pp. 1-20.

Martin, Allison M., and Lewis, W. A. "Patterns of Public Revenue Expenditures." Manchester School of Economic and Social Studies, vol. 24, no. 3 (September 1936), pp. 203-244.

Thomas, Clive Y. "Monetary and Financial Arrangements in a Dependent Monetary Economy: A Study of British Guiana, 1945-1962." *Social and Economic Studies,* Institute of Economic and Social Research, University of the West Indies, supplement to vol 14, no. 4 (Mona, Jamaica, 1965).

STATUTES

Aid to Pioneer Industries Ordinance, Trinidad and Tobago, 1950, ch. 33, no. 3.

Banking Act, Trinidad and Tobago, no. 26 of 1964.

Central Bank Act, Trinidad and Tobago, no. 23 of 1964.

Currency Act, Trinidad and Tobago, no. 3 of 1965.

Currency Act, Trinidad and Tobago, no. 3 of 1966.

Currency Amendment Act, Trinidad and Tobago, no. 23 of 1964.

Double Taxation Relief, United States of America, Canada, United Kingdom, Government Notices, nos. 163-165 of 1966.

Finance Act, Trinidad and Tobago, no. 26 of 1964.

Finance Act, Trinidad and Tobago, no. 42 of 1966.

Income Tax (in Aid of Industry) Ordinance, Trinidad and Tobago, 1950, ch. 3, no. 2.

Income Tax (Amendment) Act, Trinidad and Tobago, no. 16 of 1963.

Insurance Act, Trinidad and Tobago, no. 24 of 1966.

Insurance Company Ordinance, Trinidad and Tobago, ch. 31, no. 19.

Order-in-Council Uniting the Colonies of Trinidad and Tobago, United Kingdom, no. 94 of 1888.

Purchase Tax Act, Trinidad and Tobago, no. 1 of 1963.

The Secretary of State's Despatch and Royal Order-in-Council Constituting Tobago a Ward of Trinidad, Council Paper No. 177, United Kingdom, 1898.

Trade and Classification List, Trinidad and Tobago, 1962.

Trinidad and Tobago Act, United Kingdom, 50 and 51 Vict., Cap. 44, 1887.

Trinidad and Tobago Independence Constitution, Trinidad and Tobago, 1962.

NEWSPAPERS (TRINIDAD AND TOBAGO)
Express.
Mirror.
The Nation.
Port-of-Spain Gazette.
Trinidad Guardian.

References to tables are in italics

Abercromby, General Sir Ralph, 11, 12
Adams, Sir Grantley, 46, 52, 54
Adelantado, 9
Africa, 3, 126, 156, 157
Agriculture, 19-20, 43, 109, *110*, 161.
  See also specific areas
Aid, foreign, 136, 166, 167
Altamira, Rafael, 5
Amerindians, 3, 4
Anguilla, 29, *48*, 157, 158, 159, 163-164
Antigua, 17, *29*, 32, *48*, 165
Appliances, electrical, *67*, 68-69
Arawaks, 3, 125
Argentina, 110n
Asia, 156, 157
Asphalt, 43
Audiencias, 9
Aztecs, 125

Bahamas, 16, 32, 160
Balance of payments, 63
Bandanaraike, W.R.D., 134
Banking. *See also* British colonial
  policy; Currency
  foreign domination of, 18, 35-36,
    80-81
  reforms in, 73-83, 88-89
  central bank, 60, 79-80, 118
  Central Bank Act, 1964, 73-78, 80-83
  commercial banking, 77, 78-83, 119n,
    146
  Commercial Banking Act, 1964, 73,
    78-80, 80-83, 119n
Bank of England, 81
Bank of London and Montreal, 82
Bank of Nova Scotia, 18, 82
Barbados
  and British colonial policy, 4, 16, 17,
    26, 30-31
  and Caribbean integration, 28-29,
    160, 165
  and FWI, *48*, 50, 51, 52
  isolation of, 30
  population of, *29*
Barbuda, *29*, *48*, 163-164
Barclays Bank, 18, 82, 94, 95
Bartidos, Roderigo de, 5
Batista, Fulgencia, 128, 162, 167
Beer and ale, 65. *See also* Spirits
Bermuda, 16, 32

Berrio, Antonio de, 6
Berrio, Ferdinand de, 6, 9, 127
Better Villages Program, 143
Blair, Patricia, 157n, 158
Brain drain, 136-141, *138*
Brewster, Havelock, 162, 165
Britain
  and brain drain, 137
  capital outflow from, 90
  and Central Bank Act, 73, 76-77, 76n
  and Chaguaramas, 32-34, 52-53, 54
  and commercial banking, 79-80
  and currency, 76-77
  and double taxation, 102
  and FWI, 47, 50, 55, 57
  and Independence Constitution, 58
  and insurance reforms, 84-89
British Caribbean currency board, 118
British colonial policy, 60, 125, 126.
  See also Order in Council
  administrative, 12-16, 22, 29-32
  and *cabildo*, 11, 13, 26-27
  and communications, 30, 156
  economic, 16-19, 19-22, 35-38, 57,
    89
  judicial, 14, 15
  stated principles of, 12-16
  and taxation, 23, 69-70
  and union, 20-24
British, Dominion, Colonial, and
  Overseas Bank. *See* Barclays Bank
British Guiana, 18, *29*, 30-31, 32, 39,
  165. *See also* Guyana
British Honduras, 28, *29*, 39
Bruce, Victor, 75n
Bryan, Victor, 40
Bullionism. *See* Mercantilism
Busia, K.A., 125, 126, 142
Butler, Uriah, 32, 40

Cabildo, 10-11, 13, 26-27
Canada, 17, 86-87, 102, 110n, 137
Canadian Bank of Commerce, 18
Canadian Imperial Bank of Commerce,
  18, 82
Capildeo, Dr. Rudranath, 40
Capital gains tax, 72, 90, 99
Caribbean, 6-7, 16, 22, 28-30, 164.
  See also Caribbean integration
  communications within, 4, 24-26,
    30-31, 156, 160-161, 164, 165, 167
  future for, 146, 156-168
  industrialization of, 161